LIFE FALLS APART, BUT YOU DON'T HAVE TO:

LIFE FALLS APART, BUT YOU DON'T HAVE TO:

MINDFUL METHODS FOR STAYING CALM IN THE MIDST OF CHAOS

Julie Potiker
Foreword by Harold Kushner

ISBN: 0692977910
ISBN 13: 9780692977910
Library of Congress Control Number: 2017916973
Mindful Methods For Life Press, La Jolla, CA

ADVANCE PRAISE FOR *LIFE FALLS APART, BUT YOU DON'T HAVE TO*

"Julie Potiker turns some enormous lemons in her life into the sweetest lemonade in this wonderful book. She brings together practical brain science, powerful methods from psychotherapy, and her own friendly, funny, encouraging, and heartfelt voice to offer a wonderful roadmap and toolbox for when life throws some lemons at you."

-Rick Hanson, Ph.D., author of *Buddha's Brain: The Practical Neuroscience of Happiness, Love, and Wisdom*

"Many thanks for letting me read your lovely book. I think it captures your inspired state of mind and it's an infectious read. I'm sure many people will be touched by your work in the coming years and will be also glad to have this book to continue their learning. I'm honored to have had a role in your offering."

–Christopher Germer, PhD, author of *The Mindful Path to Self-Compassion: Freeing Yourself from Destructive Thoughts and Emotions,* and co-editor of *Wisdom and Compassion in Psychotherapy: Deepening Mindfulness in Clinical Practice*

"This book is a graceful and ebullient journey through Julie Potiker's life and the powerful practices of mindfulness and self-compassion that have sustained and transformed her. Julie's inimitable style carries you through tears, laughter, and deep gratitude for such a grounded guide through the hurricanes of our lives.

–Linda Graham, MFT, author of *Bouncing Back: Rewiring Your Brain for Maximum Resilience and Well-Being.*

"A compelling narrative packed with specific techniques patients can use to help manage the stress of everyday life."

–Paul S. Teirstein, MD Chief of Cardiology Director of Cardiology for Scripps Clinic; Medical Director of the Scripps Prebys Cardiovascular Institute for Scripps Health.

"*Life Falls Apart* is a compelling book about Julie Potiker's transformation through mindfulness and self-compassion. Julie writes with passion and humor, carrying you with her as you ride the waves of intense ups and downs, flashes of insight, and adaptive new behaviors."

–Lynne Henderson, PhD, author of *The Compassionate-Mind Guide to Building Social Confidence: Using Compassion-Focused Therapy to Overcome Shyness and Social Anxiety*

"Julie Potiker understands that we can't keep bad things from happening to us, but she offers us practical ways of making sure those bad things do not define who we are."

–Rabbi Harold Kushner, author of *When Bad Things Happen to Good People*

"Seeking the path that would lead to balance and change in her own life, Julie Potiker came upon methods, insights, and truths that were just so good for her she had to share them. This precious book is the result. Not from professional expertise or arrogance, but with the humility of being a pilgrim on the way, Julie offers riches mined from her own experience. I am sure you will find her teaching shines much light on your own path. Who could walk the way of life with such a wise woman and not emerge transformed?"

–Rabbi Alan Morinis, author of *Everyday Holiness*

TESTIMONIALS

"Julie is a natural teacher. I'd never experienced a class where the 'technologies' were imparted with such ease; no overload of information nor any need to scramble to 'get it;' rather an easy output of concepts and exercises to be 'tried on' for a size that feels right for *you*. Julie allowed us space for so many of those 'ah-ha' moments with a pacing that was slow and steady. What a wonderful experience to take this class. As the weeks proceeded, certain practices and phraseology just became part of my day whenever it was needed. For example, I found myself more often touching my heart and asking to be peaceful, safe, forgiving through-out the day—like giving myself a gift every few hours!"

    –W.S.L.

"I can feel the cortisol levels shrinking! I used to go for walks when I felt the explosions coming. Now I can do mindful walking, deep breathing or pop in a guided meditation and lock myself in my office or room. Also I appreciate opportunities for self-compassion, as I am very hard on myself. Julie, you are a gem! Your transparent, open, and honest character enhances your lessons and makes your teachings very accessible to your students. It is unusual but fabulous to be able to mix the mindfulness and meditations with a huge dose of reality, humor, and candor. We all have 'monkeys on our backs' and you created an environment that allowed us to share our issues without judgment. That's a special and unique skill."

–A.H.G.

"The retreat was an incredible and extraordinary culmination of the eight-week program. Your generosity of spirit, giving, and sharing was greatly appreciated and valued. I breathed deeper on Sunday than ever before and saw a whole new potential that I didn't know I had. Wow. You are very special and I hold this experience as a real treasure. *Todah Rabah*."

–A.H.

"I was unsure at first if meditation could really do anything for me since I am not one to sit still for long and have trouble focusing. But I have to say, learning how to take deep breaths and listen to different parts of my body as Julie is talking us all through the meditation really impacted me! I am now more aware of myself and my emotions. I am more intrigued to understand more about myself and begin to feel comfortable in my own skin. I know it's still a work in progress, but it has been a great start! Also, I loved the here-and-now stone we were given. I am very big on stones and it is great receiving one. I hold it on and off when I need a moment of relief. It's amazing how powerful a little stone can be to make one get back to being grounded. "

–B.G.

"This class surpassed my expectations. I had been holding resentment and negativity toward someone from twenty years ago. I never thought I could feel compassion or forgive this person, but it happened—and the healing I felt within my heart was amazing! Thank you so much!"

–P.C.

"Julie's way of teaching meditation is unlike any I've ever experienced before. She makes it possible for me to understand that meditation doesn't have to be done in a strict way; it's a way that we care about ourselves, and whichever way we come to it, it's always worth it. Her knowledge of so many masters and her way of synthesizing the lessons makes me feel like I've been in the stream in a deeper way. It's an absolute gift to be on this journey with her as a guide from the side."

–C.P.

"Psychologically I feel better equipped to remind myself to pause and to breathe and be more mindful during life's day-to-day challenges."

–L.P.

"I was looking for something to help me lead a more fulfilling emotional existence with less stress. I feel I've become more aware of my feelings and reactivity and find myself being more mindful. I haven't practiced twenty-minute meditations, but I find myself doing less structured mediations throughout the day."

–M.R.

"My morning meditation routine, which ends with writing my Gratitudes (which has turned into journaling), and the influence of Mindful Self-Compassion in a bunch of other ways is remarkable. I'm a happy 'mindful' camper and learning more each day."

–J.S.

"I just returned from the grocery store, and I'm really enjoying doing the Loving Kindness practice toward the strangers in the store, like in the video—it was cool!!! Thanks again, Julie! This stuff is powerful!"

–B.H.

"Thank you again for everything you did for our class. It was an amazing and life-changing experience, and I feel so blessed to have learned these tools from such a wonderful teacher. I've done a lot of 'work' in my life (therapy, coaching, workshops, seminars, yoga, etc.) and I can say that your class is truly one that will stay with me as I continue on my journey in life. It gave me tools and skills that I had never learned before and I will always have gratitude for mindfulness and self-compassion."

–C.T.

"I loved the way you treated all of us: kind, open-minded, and always supportive. I've had a shift in my outlook. I'm feeling calmer and less reactive. The program was perfect for me. It was more than I expected in terms of information and skill tutoring. I loved the style of instruction. You taught with compassion, humor, passion, and more humor! As the course progressed, I practiced almost every day. After completing the course, I can feel it in my body when I haven't taken enough time to practice. I try to meditate for fifteen minutes at least once a day. I have told my friends and others that the science and health benefits behind this practice are so intriguing."

–K.R.

"As a newer practitioner, part of the challenge is simply remembering to remember. The wristband I wear, gifted to us by Julie (our instructor) at the end of our term, says 'Self Compassion-it,' and serves as my daily reminder;

I carry with me an inner resource that can change the course of my thinking—hence my action and reaction—in a moment. I realize that when people ask me about the band or I simply glance at it, I am, in fact, practicing."
    –W.L

This book is dedicated to my family. To my husband, Lowell, who has been on the crazy roller coaster with me for the past thirty years. Our relationship nourishes my soul. To my son Michael, who grew up into a wonderful man. And to Cara and Danielle, my twin daughters, who for the last twenty years, have brought love, music, joy, sorrow, and more joy.

My Dad and my late mom have been my biggest fans. My mom showed me that you can reinvent yourself in midlife. She was a hospital administrator who began writing books in her fifties and launched a huge career for herself as a women's health author and lecturer. I don't imagine myself on the *Today* show like she was for all five of her book launches. The shoes she left me are so big that I don't envision trying to fill them. I am sad that my mom did not live long enough to see this book published. I am sure she would have been ecstatic.

I am comfortable not knowing where this book will lead me. I'm just going to stay on the roller coaster until it ends.

Allow

There is no controlling life.
Try corralling a lightning bolt,
containing a tornado. Dam a
stream, and it will create a new
channel. Resist, and the tide
will sweep you off your feet.
Allow, and grace will carry
you to higher ground. The only
safety lies in letting it all in –
the wild with the weak; fear,
fantasies, failures and success.
When loss rips off the doors of
the heart, or sadness veils your
vision with despair, practice
becomes simply bearing the truth.
In the choice to let go of your
known way of being, the whole
world is revealed to your new eyes.

Danna Faulds
(from her book *Go In and In*)

CONTENTS

FOREWORD

Julie Potiker has written an important book, a life-affirming, potentially life-changing book. At its heart is a simple but vitally important idea: you may not be able to control what happens to you in your life, but you can always control how you respond to what happens to you. You apply for a job and don't get it. It was not your fault. It may not have anything to do with your knowledge or interviewing abilities. The employer may have just been looking for someone with a different skillset. There was nothing you could have done to change the outcome. But now you have an important decision to make: how will you *choose* to respond to what happened? You could conclude that you weren't good enough and that no one will ever want to hire you. Or you can just as easily choose to believe that you are awesomely talented and capable, just not for this particular job.

Halfway through the book, Potiker quotes neuropsychologist Rick Hanson, who explains that, for evolutionary reasons, our brains tend to hold on to negative memories while forgetting positive ones. Our ancestors needed to remember past experiences of being in danger so they could be alert to possible risks in the future. Their emphasis on vulnerability and the tendency to make mistakes kept them safe. We no longer live in as dangerous a world as our primitive ancestors did. Chances are that we don't put ourselves in mortal danger every time we step outdoors. But our brains have been wired by evolution to think that is still the case. We can still be alert to people who may be out to cheat or hurt us, but most people we will encounter are not a menace. With effort, we can re-program our brains to see the world as being full of wonderful opportunities and people who can enrich our lives.

To that end, Potiker acquaints us with the virtues of Mindful Self-Compassion. You will like yourself better, and you will like other people better when you stop seeing them as competitors or threats and instead trust the world to have enough good things to nourish all of our souls. Potiker tells us how. When she and her husband experience a happy moment, she reminds herself and him to pause and fully breathe in the feeling of bliss, of beauty, of being fortunate enough to see our world at its best. By practicing this simple but profound technique, one of many that Potiker shares, they actually rewire their brains for more happiness and resilience.

The essence of Julie Potiker's message is that we have more power than we realize to define how we choose to feel about the world and the people in it. We cannot change reality, but we can choose how we feel about reality. Read *Life Falls Apart*. Absorb it. Let it do for you what it has done for its author and for so many people whom she has helped. And when you have gotten the hang of it, do what Julie Potiker has done. Share what you have gained with friends and colleagues, and let them bless you for it.

Rabbi Harold S Kushner

PREFACE

WHAT'S LOVE GOT TO DO WITH IT? A STORY ABOUT FAITH.

THREE YEARS AGO, I went to my first spirituality retreat as part of the Kivvun program run by the Institute for Jewish Spirituality. There were four components to this eighteen-month course:

1. **Yoga** (check—already doing it).
2. **Meditation** (check—big practice already).
3. **Text Study** (check, check—love it and been doing it for years).
4. **Prayer** (nope—hate it and don't do it).

Despite my resistance to even the idea of prayer, I found that when it was time for the prayer service, I sat in the back of the little space they created as a sanctuary and I cried my eyes out. Every morning until the last day, I had sheets of tears silently pouring down my face. It was if a levy had cracked in my heart and all the pain came flooding out. I couldn't get a foothold or find a metaphorical tree limb to hang onto. All of this was a complete shock to me, as I am not quick to cry in everyday life. I guess I didn't realize that trying to keep it together for the previous six years of very difficult parenting had taken such a toll on me. It's like the music in the service touched something raw and hurting, and all the stress that I thought I had been managing surged out.

One morning, between wiping all the salt water off of my face and walking to the meditation room, I took a pit stop in the restroom. Another big shock—I was bleeding. I thought I was done with all that business because I hadn't had a period in more than eighteen months.

The retreat manager went to CVS to buy feminine products for me. That night, I bled through everything. The bed and bedding looked like a murder scene from *Law and Order: SVU.*

The last time I bled like that was in 1994 when I hemorrhaged almost to death and back, after delivering my twin daughters. *Is there any relationship between that bloodletting event and this one?* I still wonder to this day. The bleeding stopped as precipitously as it began. My body let out all the blood, sweat, and tears, and then it was done.

Our brains, our minds, our hearts, and our bodies can be described as magnificent messes. I think it was around that time, after the retreat in 2012, that I realized I had stopped believing in God. I tried to trace it back, and it seemed like I lost faith around 2007 or 2008, when my twin girls were in middle school. Before that time, I was consistent about celebrating the Jewish holidays and many of the rituals in a deep way. I wrote a play for the Passover story, wrote a booklet for Sukkah, and never went out on Friday night because family Shabbat was sacrosanct. It was also definitely around the time that my girls were in middle school that my mediation practice intensified. Then, when they were in high school, practicing Mindful Self-Compassion mended the broken pieces in my heart. Did my meditation practice have anything to do with my loss of faith?

Meditation comes from the contemplative tradition of Buddhism. A Jewish atheist who believes in Buddhism is not so unusual. Many of the most beloved authors and teachers in Buddhism here in the west were raised as Jews: Rick Kornfeld, Sharon Salzberg, Joseph Goldstein, Sylvia Borstein, James Baraz, Wes Nisker, and on and on. In the 1960s, Kornfield, Bornstein, Baraz, and other Jewish spiritual seekers went to India to study and practice with Buddhist monks. I don't know whether they identify themselves with any particular religion. I just know that Judaism and Buddhist contemplative tradition can coexist beautifully. So, I wondered, maybe I'm a Jewbu?

On day six of a seven-day silent Buddhist retreat at Spirit Rock Meditation Center in Northern California, I figured something out. I am not a Buddhist. I don't believe in bowing to statues. (Thank you, Abraham.) I do believe in karma. I don't know if we are reincarnated, but it doesn't matter whether or not I know; no one knows. I want to believe that all things are connected. But I don't think everything happens for a reason. I think life is chaos.

I do believe that people can make a difference and create a better world. I believe I am my brother's and sister's keeper. And that our brothers and sisters are all humankind, not just people like us. I believe in the golden rule. Still, I am a Jewish woman who questions the existence of a higher power.

Shortly after the retreat that prompted all this questioning, I began, as I often do, putting my heart and soul into saying loving kindness phrases during meditation. It was then I realized that I was praying. Praying really hard. I have been praying for the last three years and never admitted it to myself!

May you be safe.
May you be happy.
May you be healthy.
May you live with ease.

If that's not a prayer, what is?

I've been practicing Loving Kindness Meditation (LKM) for years now. It's a great way to get that warm, openhearted feeling in your chest. Brain studies have shown significant positive changes in the brain, stemming from meditation in general and loving kindness meditation in particular. Rick Hanson, in his book *Buddha's Brain*, explains that "loving kindness mobilizes prefrontal language and intention networks as well as limbic emotion and reward networks." When you are wishing yourself or others things like safety, peace, health, and ease, you are firing neurons in your brain and installing great new neural networks. These positive mental states build up over time and result in a happier, more resilient you! But is it a prayer? When I am saying phrases for myself and others, to whom am I speaking? To myself?

There is a gorgeous children's book that I used to read to my kids when they were little called *In God's Name* by Rabbi Sandy Eisenberg Sasso, illustrated by Phoebe Stone. In the book, all these diverse people have their own name for God, and all the names are different from each other. After about a dozen characters have told the reader their names for God, they all gather around a lake. The water is still and reflective. They can each see themselves and each other reflected in the water. All at once, they say their name for God. What they hear is the word "Echad," which means "One" in Hebrew.

The meaning of this story came alive for me when I was at the Ace Hardware in Fairfax, California (a little town in Marin County near Spirit Rock Mediation Center). I was buying provisions in advance of a huge storm, predicted to be the biggest, baddest storm in twenty years.

A small, older woman came up to the register while I was checking out and asked whether she could pay for her little potted flowers at that register. It was a cute little pot with pink flowers for $4.99.

One of the nasty employees responded, "No, there is a line. A very long line."

The old woman said, "I know there is a line, but I'm ninety years old!"

The old woman started walking toward the end of the line. I caught up to her and tapped her on the shoulder, took her little flowerpot, and brought her to the register where I was checking out. She said, "That woman never should have talked to me like that. She knows me. And she knows that I've lost my husband." I told her that I was buying her flowerpot to make up for that lady making her feel bad.

We walked outside together. She hugged and kissed me three or four times. She came up to my armpit and weighed no more than ninety pounds. Her pale, brown eyes had a greenish ring around the colored part.

"Jesus sent you to me, and Jesus is blessing you right now".

"Thank you so much! I'll take that! I'll take it from Jesus, God, Buddha, and Allah. I'll take them all!" And I really meant it. I really felt it.

"Do you go to Hawaii? I have an apartment in Maui. I want you and your husband to use it." It was assumed my husband existed.

"Oh, I have no idea when and if I'd ever get there."

"What? Why, are you too proud?"

"No, not at all; it's such a nice offer. Why don't I take your name and number, and if I'm able to take a vacation in Hawaii, I'll call and ask you if your apartment is available."

"You know, I was married for sixty-seven years."

"Yes, you mentioned that. I'm so sorry for your suffering. May his memory be for a blessing." (That's totally Jewish.)

"I'm going to visit my kids. They can't pay their rent."

"It is a blessing to have kids to visit."

"Oh, I wish I could adopt you!"

"I don't think my mom would appreciate that! She's still alive and well!"

And with a twinkle in her eye she asked, "Would she be jealous?"

Walking to the car, I smiled. What a great way to end a jewel of a conversation.

After I said good-bye to the woman with the flowerpot, I returned to the Spirit Rock Buddhist Retreat Center, where they led a guided meditation on forgiveness. I teach this meditation in my secular Mindful Self-Compassion course. It is also exactly what we say in the synagogue on Yom Kippur, the holiest day of the Jewish year.

All the meditations I teach come from the spiritual contemplative tradition of Buddhism, but that doesn't make me a Buddhist. To be a practicing Buddhist, I would want to follow Buddhist rules and guides and precepts. I would want to internalize the Four Noble Truths, the Eightfold Path, and try to live my life in accordance with Buddhism. Instead, I am grateful to be able to borrow from the religion's rich, meditative tradition. Buddhists have been guiding meditations and teaching meditation for more than two thousand years. Instead, I identify myself as a spiritual seeker with a love of the healing power of Buddhist meditative practices and a strong foundation in Judaism.

Maybe Jesus sent me to that old woman, Mama Helga. But maybe God sent her to me.

In this book, I share the teachings that helped me along the path to my healing. All the teachings that have a mindfulness component, a meditation component, come from the deep well of Buddhist contemplative tradition. The teachings are universal and spiritual. At the end of this book, you will find a list of useful resources for you. Many teachers helped me on this path, and I hope that they—through their teachings, writings, and books—will help you too.

You can use this book in two ways: you can read the strategies, stories, and Mindful Methods straight through, or you can jump right to the "mindful methods" at the end of each chapter to keep you calm amid emotional chaos. Imagine a huge storm of emotion, with high winds buffeting you to and fro, and then imagine being protected under an umbrella of calm. Under this umbrella, made from the fabric of your mindfulness meditation and compassion practice, the air is light, still, and balanced.

Whether these techniques qualify as prayers and connect us to a universal force is an open question and you can answer it as you see fit. The one thing I know for sure is that they work—big time.

Over the pages that follow, you will learn about my own personal path, which I hope will help you as you navigate your own journey. Passing down stories is a time-honored tradition. Many of these stories may resonate with you because you or your loved ones may have been in similar situations. We are all in this together.

"If I am not for myself, then who will be for me? And if I am only for myself, then what am I? And if not now, when?" –Rabbi Hillel

INTRODUCTION

In 1994, AFTER eighteen weeks on bed rest trying to hang onto identical twins who were hell bent on arriving early, I gave birth to two healthy daughters. Then the nightmare began.

Unbeknownst to the doctors (and there were fifteen staff members in the operating room when the twins were delivered), uterine tissue remained on the placenta, meaning there was an open placental site. Had anyone known the tissue was still there, someone could have predicted that hemorrhaging was about to begin, and begin it did. I was bleeding to death, and I knew it. I looked at Lowell and felt filled with so much love and sorrow. To leave him with a 4-year-old boy and newborn twin girls was the saddest thing on earth. But thankfully, that wasn't my time to go. The doctors saved me. And although I was weak and albino white for a year because of the blood loss and anemia, I was on earth to be a wife, a mom, and a daughter.

Something happened that night in the operating room that set the course for the spiritual path I'm on to this day. I felt something big fill me up with peace, with a profound calm. I was floating free and light above my body. Was that God? Is there a God? Is there something out there in the universe that is a spiritual force or a supreme being? Is there a master plan in which I am playing a role?

These concerns were not typically discussed while I was growing up in Cleveland, Ohio, the third of three daughters to Ruth and Paul Jacobowitz. I was born in 1961 and my mom stayed home with me until I went to kindergarten. Then she started her career. I remember my childhood as happy.

In my sophomore year at University of Michigan, I met my husband, Lowell. We attended law school three thousand miles apart, he in Los Angeles at Pepperdine Law School, me in Washington, DC, at George Washington Law School. After graduating, we settled in Lowell's hometown, Birmingham, Michigan, near Detroit. I passed the Michigan Bar Exam and got a job at a law firm. He passed the California Bar Exam and worked in Michigan at the company founded by his parents. I had Michael, my first child, in 1990, when I was thirty years old.

After Lowell's parents sold their company in 1992, we moved to San Diego, California. I knew I wanted more children. With one son under my wing, kids seemed pretty easy. Then I got pregnant with twins.

After surviving the girls' harrowing birth, I spent the next decade doing the heavy lifting required of child-rearing. I loved being a mom of little kids. I had all the drawers in the laundry room labeled "googly eyes," "foam shapes," "markers," "crayons," "rubber stamps with ink," "paint," etc. It was like a preschool, and I was the happy but exhausted teacher. I made time to volunteer and even chaired boards of various non-profit organizations. And I was taking classes in Judaism through the Wexner Heritage Foundation, which kept me tethered to the history of my religion.

Then around the time the twins hit middle school, I went to see a neurologist named Dr. Chippendale to rule out a possible brain tumor. Why were the wrong words coming out of my mouth? "Maginal" instead of "magical"? "Capitino" instead of "cappuccino"? "Bunky-burvy" instead of "topsy-turvy"? Being with the kids really could drive a person—this person—over a cliff. One minute, everyone was getting along, and then *boom! Flash fire!* Anger and insults flying everywhere. I have never been comfortable with anger, my own or someone else's, since childhood. Anger always morphed into depression for me. Consequently, this period of my life, when my kids entered adolescence, was marked with intermittent depression. (Thank goodness I had the privilege of seeing a great therapist.)

The neurologist did a complete exam and a personal history. The diagnosis was that my brain didn't have a tumor; what it had was too much going on all the time. Three teenagers with ADHD and everything else I was doing had sent my brain into overdrive. When you are in a constant state of stress, your brain is sending cortisol and adrenaline throughout your system. As Dan Siegel points out in *Mindsight*, this chronic stress has a host of deleterious health problems.

The doctor prescribed Mindfulness Based Stress Reduction (MBSR), which is taught at hospitals all over the world. The neurologist and his wife were MBSR teachers, so he explained the health benefits of the program, and he told me to look for it at Scripps Center for Integrative Medicine in La Jolla, California, and the University of California San Diego (UCSD) Center for Mindfulness. Both were offering the course.

Jon Kabat-Zinn created MBSR in 1979 at University of Massachusetts Medical Center. Much of MBSR is taken from Vipassana meditation, which originated in Asia, and Aikido, a Japanese martial art started by Morihei Ueshiba. These techniques are steeped in traditions that are thousands of years old. Because MBSR has been used in clinical settings since 1979, it has been vetted by solid science. Solid science was and is a huge selling point for me. One of the seminal studies showing the health benefits of mindfulness meditation taught in MBSR was published in *Psychosomatic Medicine* in 2003. It indicated an increase in immune function and in activity in the part of the brain that corresponds with positive affect.

Since that study, countless other studies have revealed that MBSR decreases anxiety, depression, and blood pressure, and increases wellbeing, concentration, interpersonal relations, and the ability to manage pain.

I registered for MBSR at the UCSD Center for Mindfulness, and after eight weeks of training, I knew that a whole new world of education and practice was opening up for me. The scientific research showing the benefits of mindfulness was compelling, and the neuroscience dealing with experience-dependent neuroplasticity fascinated me. I'll get into the neuroplasticity concept more fully later on in the book, but the short version is:

What you think changes your brain.
And it doesn't stop until you are dead.

I took more than ten courses online, in several different disciplines, ranging in subjects from brain science to compassion, from overcoming obstacles to mindfulness, from awakening joy to meditation. I began learning from Rick Hanson, author of *Buddha's Brain* and *Hardwiring Happiness*, after he taught the Compassionate Brain Series for Sounds True. The Institute for Jewish Spirituality offered an eighteen-month course in yoga, meditation, text study, and prayer from the Jewish tradition. I took that too. The weeklong retreats were half in silence. The intellectual highlight for me was the study of Mussar, which is making a comeback today thanks to Alan Morinis, who wrote *Everyday Holiness* and founded The Mussar Institute. The crux of my affection for Mussar is that it deals with getting your core values in balance.

Everybody can benefit from figuring out their core values and then trying to put those values in balance. There is a nice visual image that I learned in Mussar, which explains that having a core value—called soul trait or *middah* in Hebrew—out of balance is like having a cloud covering your soul and preventing your light from shining out to the world.

Buddhism naturally emerges when studying mindfulness because mindfulness meditation is at the spiritual foundation of that religion. This may be why so many popular mindfulness and meditation teachings come from Buddhism. I felt I needed to do a more thorough investigation of the Dharma (teachings) of Buddhism. The type of practice I was taught in MBSR is completely secular. My inner nerd wanted to know where everything comes from. After spending a week at the Nyingma Tibetan Institute in Berkeley, California, my library grew exponentially. Buddhist books joined the Jewish spirituality books and the psychology and brain science books.

Five or six years after taking MBSR, the UCSD Center for Mindfulness began teaching a new curriculum written by Christopher Germer and Kristin Neff. It was called Mindful Self-Compassion (MSC), a research-proven program teaching inner resources and skills to soothe a person during times of stress or pain. Studies done on the MSC curriculum showed similar results as the studies on MBSR: decreases in anxiety, depression, and stress, and increases in relationship satisfaction, emotional wellbeing, and maintenance of healthy habits, such as diet and exercise. Mindfulness Self-Compassion was MBSR with the extra component of compassion practice. Adding a self-compassion practice gave me the capacity to take my healing to the next level. MBSR was instructive in learning how to locate emotions in my body, but not as helpful to me as MSC in handling the difficult emotions once I know how to identify them. When I say difficult emotions, I mean any emotion that doesn't feel good. Anger, frustration, sadness, grief and fear immediately pop to mind, but I'm sure other difficult emotions bubble up in people's bodies during the day.

Did you know there is something called empathy fatigue? This is how it works: compassion involves an action that will help alleviate others' pain. Empathy is feeling another person's pain. That works to some extent but gets exhausting because you are giving out and not allowing anything back in. Give, give, giving is exhausting. However, when you have compassion, you can help *alleviate* another person's pain. When you add the compassion component to your empathy, something beautiful happens: you help another person, yet in return, you experience self-compassion and self-care.

When you give and start to feel tired or drained from the giving, know that you're missing the compassion component. The feeling is real, because you can't ignore fatigue. It can take over.

I knew I wanted to become better at this so I took the class on Mindfulness Self-Compassion. It was transformative. I learned skills to soothe myself when times turn rough. My depression vanished. I managed my issues with anger much better and in a completely new way. It was such a relief that anger no longer threw me into depression. I was now comfortable telling myself, "Oh, that's anger," when it came up, because now I knew how to help myself through it. I became comfortable with getting mad at my kids and telling them I was mad and why. That was huge for me. I practiced the guided meditations on Chris Germer's website, www.mindful-selfcompassion.org, every day for years. My twins provided situations weekly, and sometimes daily, that gave me the opportunity to work with "the difficult person" meditation or many of the other meditation tools in that program.

When one of my kids was struggling during adolescence, or my mom was experiencing stress and anger because of her medical problems, I would absorb their pain and feel their frustration to the point that my level of despair would emotionally incapacitate me. After learning MSC, I knew that I had to take care of myself while I was taking care of them. I had to make time for exercise, a hot bath, a walk, and of course, meditation. Then I could be there to help in any way possible and still stay afloat.

Then, three years later, UCSD Center for Mindfulness posted that they were beginning teacher trainings for Mindful Self-Compassion, and there wasn't a nanosecond of hesitation on my part. After training with Chris Germer, Kristin Neff, and the staff at UCSD, I began teaching Mindful Self-Compassion in San Diego. It was as if everything I had been through in my life coalesced and brought me to this path.

The theatre training and the public speaking I have done for the last two decades allows me to dynamically connect with my students. The psychology I studied in college blends nicely with the self-help transformational nature of this work. My law training enables me to cut through all the psychobabble and really explain things clearly and rationally. It also makes it easy for me to teach people who are skeptical about this discipline and who think there is no way they can learn to meditate. I can clearly explain the emerging science of meditation and compassion. Living through the last eight years of parenting in one of the circles of Dante's *Inferno* makes me more approachable and gives me a wealth of material to use in class. My twin daughters recently remarked, "Mom, you should thank us for being so difficult to raise. If it had been easy, you wouldn't have built such a great tool box!"

There are fabulous scholarly books on the subjects of mindfulness, meditation, compassion, happiness, and neuroplasticity written by doctors and therapists. This book synthesizes teachings from secular mindfulness meditation, Judaism, Buddhism, neuropsychology, neurobiology, and psychology. Here you have a one-stop shop to learn what you need to know to live a balanced life. In these pages, you will learn how these methods work, why they work, and how to apply them to situations in your everyday life.

I have attached specific techniques to each of the situations described in the individual chapters. But all the techniques are applicable. Eventually, you will pick which techniques work and feel best for you.

When I started taking courses in mindfulness meditation, and attending teacher trainings and retreats, I was searching for something to help me live better in this world, to no longer be at the mercy of the "wild ride" —life's unexpected up and downs—but to respond to it with conscious intent and deliberate action. I found it. Now it's time to share it with you.

CHAPTER 1

UNHOOK YOUR PARENTING

IF I LIVED by the statement, you are only as happy as your least happy child, I would be one unhappy cookie. As a matter of fact, I was one unhappy cookie until I took my happiness into my own hands and heart and unhooked it from my kids.

Adolescence isn't easy. I wish I could have moved Dan Siegel into my house for the last eight years. He is a neuroscientist who has done wonders examining and explaining the teenage brain in his books *Brainstorm: The Power and Purpose of the Teenage Brain* (2013), *Parenting from the Inside Out* (2003), and *The Developing Mind* (1999). He extends the teenage years into a person's mid-twenties, when the front part of the brain becomes fully myelinated. Before that time, humans are impulsive and do not foresee the consequences of their actions very well. That is why kids do such dumb things.

Every parent has nightmare stories about their kids during the teen years. I just happen to have more than my share. I was blessed with identical twin girls, but cursed that I would have two females going through adolescence, at the same time, under the same roof.

My girls could be a source of such joy one minute, and then, just like that, they could start a vicious fight—really turning on a dime. So I never felt safe that I could have a good day, or a good night, without some volcanic eruption. Amazingly, they could actually behave badly in public or while friends were over at the house. They had no shame bitching each other out in front of other people. I'm sure they will not enjoy reading this, but they can't deny it, and frankly, they have it coming.

You are probably thinking, "Wow, what an incompetent parent this is! Why the heck can't she control her children? What is wrong with her?" I've often thought those same things about myself. Finally, after years of therapy, meditation, yoga, and finally Mindful Self-Compassion, I can tell you that *it is not my fault*. I did everything I could possibly do, and more than most women would probably do.

I took away things that were important to them in their world, like their cell phones, laptops, and anything else they held dear. That was a pain to monitor because homework was often done on their laptops, so I had to police that system. It was much easier when one of those harsh sentences came down in the summer when school was out! Then I could lock up their computers and they would miss all the fun computer games they loved to play.

I remember one summer all they had was a guitar, a record player and my old records; every electronic device we owned had been removed from their lives as a punishment. I grounded them so many times I lost count. One summer, my husband and I forced them to do community service three days a week. (The upside of that consequence for bad behavior was that they really enjoyed working with the seniors at the community center.) You name it, I tried it. And all the time I acted with love. To this day, they will tell you they never hated me and that they know I'm a great mom who never hated them. So that's better than some families whose kids hate their parents for a few years!

Lest you think I only have twin girls to provide me with all this teaching, as you recall from the beginning of the book, I also have a son, Michael, who was four years old when the twins were born. I can tell you, he's only now getting over the shock and intrusion of those little sisters who shattered his world.

As any mother of twins will attest, you can't go *anywhere* with two babies without every stranger in the vicinity coming up to you to look, coo, and ask questions. "Do they run in your family?" Sometimes they even reach out and try to touch the babies. (That's where a good block comes in handy!)

Michael would just stand there, like chopped liver, and after all the fuss was dying down, he'd say, "Hey, I'm the big brother!" It must have been really tough for him, and looking back, I feel compassion for that little guy. He felt his basic needs to be seen, heard, and loved were not being met. No amount of parental love and attention seemed to fill him up. So honestly, he became a monster brother to his little sisters.

He was always especially kind and caring and polite in school and in public, but oh man, he was a little devil to his sisters in private. I had to threaten to send him to a wilderness program if he didn't stop bullying his little sisters. (I had every frigging wilderness program saved and bookmarked on my laptop.) He only avoided going to a wilderness program due to my husband, who reminded me that every decision can have unintended consequences and that we might send him away for sibling rivalry and get him back as a felon!

So then his abuse became psychological. And he became the master at it. Michael is so brilliant. We had his psychological educational testing done every three years because of his ADHD, his verbal scores were always off the charts. His ability to use his speech as a weapon was intense. He could pick just the right insult to cut those little sisters to the quick.

When he was being nice, like offering to drive the girls to the mall, he was charging them exorbitant rates for his services and taking advantage of their cluelessness about the value of money. I found this out just recently, in a family therapy session with Danielle. She said Michael charged them so much that she claims he took half of the money they received as gifts for their bat mitzvahs. I asked him about it the other night, and he laughed and said they must have taken in a pretty small haul if that was half their money! It's all pretty much water under the bridge now that they are all in their twenties. They can sit around the kitchen table, laughing and joking like friends. But believe it or not, I still have scars from their sibling rivalry!

You might be wondering why I didn't contact professionals at the time, to help me manage all this chaos. Well, of course I got help! Michael told me when he was ten years old that his therapist was a buffoon. Michael warned me that it would take years of him sitting on the floor and playing with dirty, broken action figures, before the doctor would be able to tell me anything about my son. I suggested at the time that he sit in a chair, like the little man he was, and discuss issues with said buffoon to see if that made any difference. Nope, once a buffoon, always a buffoon. (Interesting postscript: twelve years later, I had occasion to interact with that same therapist, and I concluded that Michael was right!)

When the twins were in middle school, they begged to return to a particular summer camp they had attended when they were younger. They thought, now that they were 14, that Rock Star Camp, where kids learn to write, record, and perform songs, would be even more fun. They thought they would write and record new, more young adult material. After all, they were both incredibly talented singers and songwriters, so why wouldn't it be a success?

When they got there, they called and said, "It's awful. There's no kids our age. We want to come home." After calling the camp and finding out there were plenty of kids their age, I told them they would have to make the best of it and we would see them at the end of camp. "The first couple of days are always an adjustment. You have each other." You get the picture. I was firm and loving.

The following day, I received a phone call from the infirmary at the camp. The nurse informed me that I needed to come pick up my children, saying, "The camp is not equipped to deal with a situation such as this."

"What situation?"

"Your daughters are both threatening to commit suicide if they have to stay at camp. We're sorry, but we just can't keep them."

Oh my God! Really?

I had a psychiatrist who knew them (not the buffoon) call them at the infirmary, and even he couldn't get them to change their tune. So I sent their brother Michael to drive up and get them. I was so pissed by their behavior I didn't even want to see their faces. We told our son that

6

he should explain to the girls that the police would meet them at the front of the psych hospital where they'd be admitted that night. We told him to tell them we would see them when they got to the hospital. It was only when they thought they were being admitted to a psych ward that they came clean and said they'd made it up. *Can you believe it!* That was the summer they had no privileges. Whatsoever.

It could always be worse though. I've heard stories that are way scarier than the twins' summer camp escapade. I even have some, but I'll give my kids a break for a while and share other people's heartaches.

BILL AND MARY

In their high school years, the mistakes kids make can have greater than average impact. They are supposed to be staying in school, doing their work toward graduation, and getting ready for college. Our friends Bill and Mary have a son named Mark who seemed to have the opposite in mind. One day, the principal at Mark's school called to say that Mark just stood up in the middle of class and walked out.

It turned out that Mark had a problem with marijuana. His problem was moderation. Every kid in high school in California knows someone with a medical marijuana card. If they want pot, they can get it. And the pot is strong. It's not like the pot in the sixties and seventies.

I have seen medical grade pot and edibles labeled at over 24 percent THC. And all the kids say it's not addictive and that it is not a gateway drug. Guess what, kids? Pot that strong *can* be addictive and it *can* be a gateway drug.

Bill and Mary have what most people would consider a wonderful family life. Their children go to a good school, and they live in an upscale neighborhood in Orange County, California. On the day the principal called to say they needed to come in to have an important discussion, they confronted Mark about it. To their shock, Mark admitted right then and there, that he needed to go to rehab. He explained that he needed to get away from his current environment to clean up his act. Mary got on the Internet and researched the world of addiction and residential rehab centers.

One of her close friends had, unfortunately, been through this already with her own son, so she was a great resource to Mary, who was terrified. She found a spot about an hour north of home and reserved a bed for Mark. She went shopping to get him what he'd need—an electric razor instead of straight razor, no toiletries containing alcohol, etc. She kept bursting into tears at the thought that she wouldn't be able to protect him. Mary spent days agonizing over her decision. She was confused, disappointed and scared; but worst of all, heartbroken. It's devastating to find out your kids have lied to you, even though it's fairly common for teenagers to lie to their parents. Mary wasn't looking at the situation as right or wrong, she was looking at it from her own idea of what it meant about her relationship with her children.

When she tried to imagine what his days would be like at the rehab, how difficult it would be for her son, she came undone. She knew she couldn't protect him. He would be all on his own.

Mary had to explain everything to Mark's school principal and teachers when she withdrew him. The night before he left, Mark had a party to say, "Good-bye, I'm going to rehab," to all his friends. It seemed surreal to Mary, like he was using the situation to create celebrity. Then, at midnight, he went into Bill and Mary's room and said he couldn't go to rehab in the morning. He claimed he wanted to try withdrawing on his own; after all, he hadn't tried stopping on his own yet.

By now, he had effectively manipulated his parents into withdrawing him from school to go to rehab, and now he had to be home schooled because his high school knew he was a drug addict. Or, she thought, maybe he wasn't really a drug addict. Maybe he just wanted to avoid getting up and going to school altogether. He often said, "Wow, school is so boring, you just have no idea."

Either or? It didn't seem to occur to Mary that her son could be both a drug addict and lazy.

Mary was slow to reach the conclusion that she and her husband were being played by their son. Instead they reacted helplessly to the succession of Mark's antics: Bill was angry. Mary was crushed. She felt overwhelmed and weakened by the devastating emotions she felt, one right after the next.

They also felt they let Mark down, and themselves, by not being stronger, savvier parents. They felt terrible for themselves and inadequate in their parenting role.

They ultimately reasoned that the only way to make this traumatic situation okay in their heads and hearts was to let go and give themselves compassion. They realized the situation was a mess, but once things settled down into a routine, with Mark working at home with a teacher, and Mary going back to work, the gym, yoga and spending time with her friends, Mary let go of being ashamed of both her son and herself. She practiced techniques to separate herself from the actions of her son, so she could regain her equanimity.   Bill didn't seem to have as difficult of a time as Mary, because he didn't feel that Mark's actions reflected poorly on him as a father. He knew he wasn't at fault, so giving himself compassion came easier to him than Mary.

MINDFUL METHODS FOR STAYING CALM AMID EMOTIONAL CHAOS

1. The Receiving-Sending Meditation

The background on this practice is part of what makes it so remarkable. The Receiving-Sending

Meditation is essentially Tonglen Meditation, attributed to Atisha Dipankara Shrijnana, who lived and taught Buddhism in the tenth century in India. It involves breathing in the bad, and breathing out the good. Pema Chodron, a phenomenal teacher of Tibetan Buddhist thought and practice, has written many books explaining how to have less suffering and more ease in your life. Her book *Tonglen*, written in 2001, is a thoughtful endorsement of this ancient practice. Tara Brach also has popularized this practice and has a wonderful YouTube video leading Tonglen meditation. The specific methods can vary, but the basic idea is to breathe in the suffering, and breathe out relief. It sounds counterintuitive, but it works. The Receiving-Sending Meditation also can work by breathing out the suffering. Either way is fine. It is the intention of your focused attention that allows the meditation to be effective.

This happens to be my favorite meditation. It works in so many different situations. You can do it in a formal sitting meditation, or snap into it on the spot. If I see someone suffering, I automatically breathe in their pain, and the pain of others in their situation, and breathe out light or love or peace. Making a decision to do something like concentrating on my breath with a visualization of others in the same situation connects me to a sense of common humanity. Imagining suffering morphing into peace helps calm my system. You will see how it can help you in the exercise below.

Practicing the Receiving-Sending Meditation

Get in a comfortable position, sitting with your back relatively straight and relaxed. Close your eyes gently. Take three deep, nourishing breaths. Find your breath where you notice it most easily. It may be the bottom of your nostrils, your chest, or your belly. Tune in to your breath. Watch your breath for a few minutes. Notice what's going on in your body. Given the two parenting stories above, the story of my kids at camp and Mark's story, parents in these situations might be feeling frustration, anger, disappointment, shame, fear, worry, hopelessness, and depression.

See if you can pinpoint in your body where those emotions are manifesting themselves. Emotions are funny things. You can have many emotions at the same time. In fact, they can be a tangled mess. When you quiet down long enough, you can tease apart the different emotions. Here's how to do it:

Name the emotion and locate it in your body. Keep in mind that underneath surface emotions are usually other, more tender emotions. For instance, you may feel anger, but if you probe deeper, you may find fear. Underneath fear is shame, underneath shame is a core unmet need—like the need to be seen, heard, loved. So your inner dialogue might be like this:

"Oh, that's anger in my stomach."
"Oh, that's shame under the anger."
"Oh, that's depression in my heart."

See if you can visualize what the anger, shame, or depression looks like. Is it like a cinder block? Is it hot or cold? Is it shaky or still? Is it contracting, like pulling in and down?

Then, breathe in the pain. Drive your breath into the place you feel it most.

Focus your attention on your intake breath, and breathe it right into the pain.

There is a space in between your intake breath and your outtake breath. Visualize that gap as a huge cavern filled with light. Your pain is dropping down into that space. Your pain is not alone. You are breathing in the pain of all the people in the world who are experiencing the same suffering right at that moment. Millions of people are suffering just like you right now. Millions of people are suffering from worse incidents, and millions of people are suffering from lesser incidents.

The pain coming in gets transformed by something in the cavern, so that your out breath is a light, free breath of ease, goodwill, and freedom from suffering. Breathe in the pain; breathe out clear goodness. In goes the shame; out goes the peace. In comes the anger; out the goodwill. Keep practicing for fifteen minutes, and then let the last five minutes be free from focusing your attention on your breath, words, or feelings. Just sit with your eyes closed and notice what comes up, allowing your experience to be just what it is.

The Receiving-Sending Meditation can help you get rid of toxic emotions, so you can feel better. Your child's misdeeds do not figure into this equation. You are taking care of you. The outrage and fear that you feel after a big screw-up by one of your kids festers inside, and if you don't let it out, it turns into a monster. Some parents let it out by screaming at their kids, but that doesn't work, and it usually causes more anger and shame. Other parents disconnect to try to avoid the pain, or they numb the pain, but that doesn't work either, and it adds the pain of disconnection to all the other pain. If you can morph those bad feelings into good feelings, or at least light and neutral feelings, you will be doing your body a world of good. There is a bit of wisdom that says that anger corrodes the vessel that contains it. You are that vessel.

Once you are not feeling hot with emotion, you will be less reactive with your child and deal with the facts on the ground. The reality of whatever happened or didn't happen needs to be handled—this isn't a free pass to blow off parenting. Instead, it will hopefully allow laying down a boundary or a consequence feel easier, like it is coming from a place of calm inside you.

Mark's parents were disgusted that they got snookered by their manipulative and lazy child. They needed to learn how to forgive themselves, and practicing the Receiving-Sending Meditation helped them. They also needed to forgive Mark, which took longer for Mary longer than Bill. She is more of a grudge carrier than her husband. But with her Mindful Methods tool box, and years passing where the memory of the anger and shame faded, she forgave Mark. She didn't forget, but she did forgive.

2. Here-and-Now Stone

Use an object to ground you. In my classes, students pick a polished stone from a bowl, and that becomes an object on which they can focus their attention. Select a stone from your yard, a craft store, the beach, or a garden store. Choose the stone that calls to you if you have a big assortment. For my classes, I purchase gorgeous, polished, colored stones on a website called Rock Tumblr.

Once you have your stone, spend a few moments really looking at it. Notice the range of colors, textures, and temperature of the stone. Rub your fingers on the stone. Move the stone around in your hand. Think about the fact that the stone might be billions of years old. While you are focusing your attention on the stone, guess what you are not thinking about? You are not thinking about the past or the future! You are not going down the rabbit hole of a story line about how awful your situation is because of whatever mess you are slogging through right now. You are focused on your stone, thereby giving your brain a much-needed break from the chaos. This is a positive distraction to separate yourself from the mess that makes you feel like you are under an avalanche. The stone is like the opening that allows you to breath through the small hole in the snow. It helps you calm down until you can figure out the best way to dig yourself out entirely.

Those emotional snowstorms adopt many guises. Any parent who has taken their young child to the grocery store knows that just making your way through the gauntlet of tantalizing items in the cereal aisle can be an exhausting ordeal. And let's not even talk about the toy aisle at the drug store! When I think back, I have left countless shopping carts filled with merchandise at Target. They never neared the checkout counter because I had to grab my misbehaving children and march out of the store to my car. Danielle once had a tantrum at Stride Rite because she wanted Jellys, but her feet were too narrow for those clear rubber sandals. I never took her back to Stride Rite—ever. And she never got Jellys.

Sometimes you cannot physically break from negative momentum because you might be trapped in your car. One of my students was driving her ten-year-old son, and he was giving her all the reasons why he had to have a new skateboard. He had to have this specific one. She suggested if he wanted it so badly, he should work to save up money to purchase it. He said that would take too long and that he wanted it now. She said that it wasn't his birthday or a holiday, and just because he wanted something didn't mean he was going to get it. While she was talking, she was simultaneously rifling around in her purse for her stone.

Her son asked her what the heck she was doing.

She told him she was holding her here-and-now stone and that it made her feel better.

He said, "Wow, Mom, you have an anger management problem."

Of course, the truth is that the stone and her mindfulness practices are why she doesn't have an anger management problem! Her kid was having a bratty moment and her stone let it roll off her back. She didn't go down the rabbit hole in her mind worrying that she was raising a bratty, entitled child who would grow up to be an obnoxious adult.

One of my students has a difficult relationship with her sister. Whenever she has to talk to her, she keeps her here-and-now stone in her hand. She explains that her stone makes her less reactive and serves as a nurturing reminder to be good to herself. That is a beautiful example of the importance of intention.

Here-and-now stones are excellent in the workplace. Keep one on your desk and let it be your reminder to ground yourself. Carry the

stone in your pocket when you go into meetings. You may be surprised at how much calm
support you feel and how clearly you can think
even under stress. Even if you are dealing with
difficult personalities or problematic tasks,
you can reach in your pocket, feel your stone
and it reminds you to pause and breath. This
gives you the space to have more thoughtful,
skillful reaction to any set of circumstances.

3. **Self-Care: Do what gives you joy.**
   The mindfulness exercises in this book do
   double duty when they are also the activities
   that bring joy. I love Brené Brown's definition of a joyful life from her book, *The Gifts
   of Imperfection.* She writes, "I believe a joyful
   life is made up of joyful moments gracefully
   strung together by trust, gratitude, inspira-
   tion, and faith." These joyful moments are everyday events, like waking up in a warm bed,
   enjoying your first cup of coffee in the morning, and looking out the window.

   Think of all the things that give you joy.
   Brainstorm with yourself and take a moment
   to list as many things you can think of, even
   little things like a soft pillow to sleep on and
   talking to your best friend. Live music is a big
   joy-giver for me, so I have live music on my list.

Look at your list first thing in the morning, and set your intention to do something from your joy list that day. Look at the list at night and review what you did from the list and how it made you feel. You will notice how your outlook improves when you are giving yourself specific experiences that give you joy.

James Baraz, in his *Awakening Joy* course and book of the same name, uses Buddhist teachings to help people live happier lives. He and Rick Hanson agree that we should "take in the good" of a wholesome state when we have one, and that we should actively create wholesome states. Then, they recommend we let it really land in our bodies for a breath or two, so we can counteract our negativity biases and rewire our brains for happiness.

I remember talking to a close friend, Sarah, who was going through a rough financial transition in her life. I asked her what gave her joy. Together we made a list of her responses. On the list were fresh flowers, live music, time with friends and family, yoga, warm baths, and good books. We talked about taking a look at that list every couple of days and trying to fit one of those items into her day. Just creating the list and revising it from one month to another made her happy. She felt like she was taking control of her happiness. After a week of remembering to pick up flowers on her way home from work, she reported feeling in better spirits. Then, while on a business trip in Las Vegas, she remembered that live music was on her list, so she bought a ticket to a Rod Stewart concert and loved every minute of it!

As she grew more comfortable with focusing on things that gave her joy, she started thinking about expanding her horizons, or her lists, to things that "could or might" give her joy. She planned a cruise, wanting to expand what she began to view as a fairly "limited or predicable list." Her activities and interests grew as her lists became more varied. Today she's a happy well-rounded person.

We all need to take control of our happiness. Otherwise we may be buffeted by all the negative emotions that happen when things don't go as we hoped. We can choose to be happy. We can plan our happiness!

A plan for happiness can act as a positive touchstone when life takes a petrifying turn. I asked for and received permission from my daughter Danielle to tell the following story. She said if sharing her troubles could help even one person, that she believed it was worth it to share her business.

A few years ago, I was flying back to San Diego from Detroit. It was evening, I had used airline points to purchase the ticket, and I was sitting comfortably in the first-class cabin, sipping a glass of red wine. A man in his fifties sat next to me. We started chatting, and one story lead to the next. Suddenly we were connecting, sharing very personal and painful parts of our lives.

Something going on with one of his kids was torturing him. He was one of those Fortune 500 guys, masters of the universe, but he was cut off at the knees by the unspeakable truth that his teen daughter was hurting herself. His daughter was "cutting." It was difficult for him to even say the words. He felt the power of shame. I remember him trying to explain it without that exact phrasing, and I remember how out of his depth he looked when he finally said "cutting."

When I put my hand over my mouth and said, "Oh my God, I'm so sorry. I know what you are going through; it happened in my family," he was visibly relieved. It was as if he had been holding his breath for months and could finally exhale.

We talked about all the emotions that come up with this sort of horror. Shame and anger jump to mind immediately. And under those hot emotions are often softer emotions like fear and confusion. Below the fear and confusion might be a feeling of being unworthy or unlovable. I flashed back to a time three years prior when my husband called me to say, "Things are out of control, honey. You've got to come home." After examining the inside of my daughter's lower arm, I drove her to the emergency room. I didn't know whether she needed stitches for any of the lacerations. My parents were with me when my husband called, so I told them where I was headed and they met me in the emergency room. My mom was a hospital administrator my whole childhood, so there was no stopping them from being there for Danielle and me.

It is heartbreaking to see your child hurting. And seeing one of your own children so visibly hurting, scarring herself, is crushing. I have a memory, an image, of sitting up on the exam table next to her after the doctor put glue on some of her cuts. My head hung low, the weight of the situation oppressive. My parents were sitting in chairs facing us. They looked exhausted and pale. I was bleeding inside, and Danielle was bleeding outside. I was so sorry to be sharing this pain with my parents. They didn't need this in their lives. And even though I didn't have all the coping tools then that I have now, I knew enough to be able to recognize and label everything going on inside me. The list looked something like this: worry and fear, followed by failure, shame, and hopelessness.

Sitting there, head hanging low, next to my beautiful and talented cut-up girl, I wanted to shrivel up and die. I didn't think I was strong enough to pull her through this, and I was frankly too tired to think about what was going to happen tomorrow. I was so ashamed to be sitting there in front of my parents like this, with all the stuffing taken out of me. I know they weren't judging me, but they are my parents who love me, and I knew it was breaking their hearts seeing not only Danielle like this, but me like this. Even though I'm a grown-ass woman, I'm still their child.

I soon learned that cutting is unfortunately not unusual. I read everything I could get my hands on to try to wrap my head around what we were dealing with. Kids who engage in this behavior do so, on average, between ages twelve and sixteen years old. In the United

States and Canada, the prevalence ranges from 12% to 41% in community samples of adolescents and young adults. For youth receiving mental-health treatment, some studies suggest that as many as 40% to 60% of young adults and adolescents self-injure. (*Journal of Mental Health Counseling*, October 2011) Cutting isn't the only way these kids hurt themselves; it was just the way *my* kid was hurting herself. But other parents have witnessed their kids banging their heads into walls, burning themselves, pulling their hair, biting themselves, picking their wounds, breaking their bones, and swallowing toxic substances.

Cutting is called nonsuicidal self-injury (NSSI) in the therapeutic community. NSSI is the "deliberate destruction or mutilation of one's own body tissue without the conscious intention to die." In the resources section at the back of this book, I suggest a good article from the *Journal of Mental Health Counseling* from October 2011, which addresses NSSI and discusses how compassion-focused therapy (CFT), developed by Paul Gilbert and his colleagues (Gilbert & Irons, 2005, Gilbert & Procter, 2006), can be an effective methodology to work with people who hurt themselves. CFT starts with mindfulness and has roots in neuroscience, evolutionary psychology, and Buddhist teachings.

So there I was, sitting next to this man who just had all the stuffing taken out of him, and I had absolute empathy. And I had knowledge. And I had hope for him because we had already made it out the other end of that nightmare. Cutting was just a troubling memory in our lives, not a current source of fear and anguish. What a blessing that the universe put us together that night. He and I communicated by e-mail a couple of times after that, and then we drifted apart.

I know it was embarrassing for the man on the plane to share all he did with me about his daughter, because he told me that not one other person in his life, except for his wife, who was absolutely bereft, knew about what they were going through.

Brené Brown has spent her professional life studying shame. In her book, *The Gifts of Imperfection* (2010), she defines shame as "the intensely painful feeling or experience of believing that we are flawed and therefore unworthy of love and belonging."

When I learned how to work with my shame and forgive myself, I healed myself. That doesn't mean that I don't feel shame anymore or that I don't feel anger or anxiety or fear. It means that I feel those negative emotions at a deep level and am able to work with them and find a balance in my life, with all the suffering and joy that life entails. Pema Chodrun, one of the most amazing teachers of Buddhist practice, sums it up like this: "We can still be crazy after all these years. We can still be timid or jealous or full of feelings of unworthiness. The point is not to throw ourselves away and become something better. It's about befriending who we are already."

We can choose to disconnect our ability to experience joy from the actions of our offspring. When I began to realize that I could have a good day, even if my kids were having a bad day, it changed my life. Of course, I have sympathy for them if they are sad or in trouble. And I usually have tremendous compassion for their situations. I can give them my shoulder to cry on and listen and hold them in my arms. I can watch funny movies with them to try to help them change the channel in their minds. I can help them view things from different perspectives. And I can lead them in guided meditation and guided visualization.

I'll also do whatever I can to provide the re-sources that might help them. If they need a professional, a tutor to help with schoolwork or a psychologist or psychiatrist, I'll make it happen. But I can still have a good day, and a good life, even if they are unhappy.

Stefani, Putting it All Together.

Stefani came to me upset. Her son had gotten kicked out of high school for the second time for drinking at a school dance. She was anxious with worry, fear and shame. After I made sure she had a good relationship with a therapist, I took her on as a client to teach her mindfulness medita-tion and compassion practice. The Receiving-Sending Meditation that worked so well for me, Mary and Bill resonated with her. Twice a week for four weeks, we met and practiced it. She vi-sualized breathing in the pain of all the moms in the world who were upset or disappointed in their kids. She breathed in all the pain, breathed it into a vast space inside of herself, and breathed out light and love into a vast ocean. She visu-alized the pain as dark, thick smoke when she breathed it in, and then light and peace when she breathed out. The sense of spaciousness was very healing for Stefani. She told me she felt less alone and also lighter after we practiced the

Receiving-Sending Meditation together. She felt connected to all the other moms in the world whose pain was now mingling with her own. That sense of loving connected presence is a wonderful buffer to the isolation that was leading her to depression.

Stefani chose a here-and-now stone from my bag of stones and kept it with her at all times. Whenever her thoughts started to spiral downward, she grabbed her stone and zoned in on the color and texture of her stone. She kept it in her pocket during the day and on her nightstand at night. It worked for her because she could focus her attention on the stone. When her attention was on the stone, she wasn't dwelling on the troubles with her son.

At our first session, I suggested that Stefani make a list of all the things that give her joy. Then twice a week, when she came in for her session, we went over the list, and she shared what she had managed to do each day that made her day a little better. Some of her items were easy to do, like taking a bath with lavender bath salts. She started a nightly bath ritual and even added candles and her favorite music to her bath experience. She also made sure she made it to yoga class at least twice a week and that she took a walk at least twice a week. Her favorite walking spot is a state park in San Diego called Torrey Pines State Reserve. She feels like she's connected to something bigger when she is standing high up on the cliffs, looking out at the ocean. And the ocean is the visual that she uses during the Receiving-Sending Meditation when she imagines breathing out into the vastness of the sea.

Stefani is doing really well. She is happy and healthy and continues with her therapy. She wishes things were going more smoothly with her son, but she is dealing with the fact that things don't always go the way we wish them to be, and she is okay with that reality. One day I told her that the Buddha said we make our own hell by wishing things were different than they are. She said, "I'm over that. What will be, will be!"

MINDFUL METHODS TO UNHOOK YOUR PARENTING

*The Giving and Receiving Compassion Meditation. This can be done in many ways and in many situations. To unhook your parenting, I would recommend one of two ways. You can breathe compassion in for yourself and out for the other person who is hurting, whether it is your teenager, yourself or another parent. You can also breathe in the other person's suffering and the suffering of all the people in your situation (including yourself) and breathe out peace and light. You can even breathe in the suffering of all the teenagers who are in trouble and breathe out peace and light.

*Use your here-and-now stone every day. You'll see the here-and-now stone used a lot as a Mindful Method in this book. Choose a stone for yourself. I have a here-and-now stone on a chord around my neck. I also have one in my purse that my daughter Cara bought for me. It has a cool mother-energy symbol cut into it. I find myself reaching up for the stone on my necklace and rubbing it between my fingers on and off during the day. It's nice if you have your stone somewhere that you can reach it easily. I know some people keep theirs on a shelf in their closet so they can put it in their pocket each day. I keep the stone that my daughter Cara bought for me in the outside pocket of the purse that I carry every day. When you are focused on your here-and-now stone, you are in the present moment and not worrying about your child's past or future.

*Make a list of what gives you joy and do something on that list for yourself daily. I cannot recommend this highly enough. You only have to write the list once, unless you, like Sarah did earlier, discover new things that bring you joy along the way. When you are feeling joy, remember to let it fill you up for a few breaths so that you are installing that positive mental state and rewiring your brain for more happiness and resilience!

CHAPTER 2

BETRAYAL: BE YOUR OWN BFF

BEING YOUR OWN best friend involves loving yourself. Loving yourself always involves self-compassion, and self-compassion involves self-care. A lack of self-care can leave you feeling unlovable. You can find it difficult to connect—which as human primates we are hardwired to do—and that disconnection can lead to depression. If you believe you are not enough—not smart enough, accomplished enough, thin enough, rich enough—then you may not be able to cope when the emotional shit really hits the fan, especially in a marriage or partnership—when the stakes are very high.

How many couples will find out *today* that their partner is cheating on them? If you look at divorce statistics here in the United States, it adds up to plenty of heartbreak. In the United States, according to the American Psychological Association, 90% of people marry for the first time by age 50 and 40% to 50% of first marriages end in divorce. For subsequent marriages, the rate of divorce goes up. It's true some marriages fail for other reasons-incompatibilities which have nothing to do with cheating—but cheating is a huge reason why relationships fall apart. And lives and families fall apart if the infidelity leads to a break up.

I wonder what happens after your trust is shattered. I've heard friends in this situation ask questions such as:

- What does love mean anyway?
- Can someone who professes love be capable of cheating?
- How long is it going to take to feel just a little less shitty?
- Why me?
- Why not me?
- Oh my God, is this ever going to stop? Am I ever going to feel like myself again?

Before my training and practice, I used to wonder how to support my friends and loved ones who were having their hearts ripped out and lives devastated by divorce. Now, I can offer them concrete advice for taking care of themselves.

DEBORAH

My friend Deborah came home early from work one day to find a woman walking out of her bedroom. Yes,

Deborah's husband was right behind this hussy. (Oops, I called her a hussy! Yes, I did! That is not right. But it does show my humanity!) I know she may be the instrument of the wreck, but the husband is the home wrecker. That woman, an acupuncturist, was single, so she wasn't breaking any vows. The broken vows were his.

Deborah and Mitch had been married for more than thirty years, and she thought they were happy. Sure, they both worked hard. Yes, he came home from the office late and was often tired, but that never sent up a red flag. Deborah had always been a mellow person, but this scene flipped a switch in her that she didn't even know she had, and she went berserk. She was shocked at the scene and shocked at herself. What the hell did Mitch think he was doing?

It turned out Mitch was "doing" this woman for years. This totally pulled the rug out from under Deborah. She called me late at night, crying and describing searing pain zinging around her body, as if her nervous system were on fire.

Deborah went to a doctor, a therapist, and an acupuncturist—not *that* acupuncturist—to try to calm her system down. She worked full-time, so she was also keeping it together at work and keeping it together for her daughters. She and her husband separated and then divorced. To this day—and it has been years since the emotional hurricane struck her life—she has never divulged her husband's infidelity to her kids. I know that's what all the books say to do, but I couldn't imagine having the strength and grace to keep my husband's reputation clean if I were in her shoes.

Deborah spent years and years building a new life—a great life, but not anything like she had planned. All that rebuilding takes tremendous energy and effort. Deborah is a bastion of courage and brainpower, but I know there were times she wanted to curl up and quit. I know it because she told me, and I didn't blame her one bit.

When major events happen in the lives of her children, Deborah has to face that man who broke her heart and crushed her soul. I was a guest at her daughter's quinceañera, a fabulous "coming out" party for Latin American girls, signifying their transition from childhood to womanhood. I watched her, filled with grace and equanimity, floating through the event as if from above. She has a wonderful man in her life now. Ten times the man her husband morphed into at midlife. This new man shares her values and ethics. That, in the end, is what it's all about.

It's painful to listen to a dear friend's grief and feel like you have nothing to offer. I know that sometimes just bearing witness to the suffering is enough, and sometimes that is best. But because I am a fixer, it makes me more comfortable being able to add compassion to my empathy. Compassion is wanting to alleviate her suffering; it requires action. It's not the same as empathy, stepping into her shoes and feeling her pain. I wish I had the education back then to do more than just listen.

What I would have told Deborah if I had known then what I know now? On those nights when she was lying alone in bed, crying with pain zipping around her body, a body scan might have helped.

Do a body scan. I first learned the body scan in MBSR, but it is based on a Buddhist meditation. Pick a body-scan guided meditation from any YouTube video or from the Insight Timer App (please see the Resources section of this book).

In this meditation, you are laying on your back, arms at your sides. Start at the toes on your left foot, and bring your attention there. Relax your left toes, then your foot, your ankle and then slowly make your way up your left leg. Then you start over with the toes on your right foot, your foot, ankle, calf, knee, and thigh. You might feel a tingling sensation wherever you are directing your attention. You will notice that as you relax one part of your body, the other parts get easier.

Eventually you get to your pelvis, the trunk of your body, shoulders, up and down each arm, then the neck and head. When you get to your head, imagine relaxing the back of your neck. Let that feeling of relaxation roll up the back of your head to the top of your head, then down your forehead and face. If you get to a part of your body where you have pain, see whether you can label the emotion where the pain is. Then imagine putting a warm compress or rubbing soothing oil on that area. You can intentionally try to soften that spot while you are imagining the soothing oil on it.

You also can thank your body parts for doing such a good job for you. Your body does its thing all day, running its circulatory and skeletal systems without any assistance from you! I thank my feet for holding me up all day!

At the end of the body scan, if you are still awake, you should feel a sense of calm all over your body. People always ask whether they are meditating if they are sleeping. No, you are sleeping if you are sleeping! But that is fine! Sleeping is good! The body scan meditation usually puts me to sleep so I use it as a sleep aid.

Say loving kindness phrases. Create phrases you can say over and over again while meditating that will make you feel good. Ask yourself what basic needs are not being met right now that are causing this suffering. The need to be loved? The need to be safe? The need to be understood? Then take those needs and turn it into a phrase such as:

> *May I know that I am loved;*
> *May I be safe;*
> *May I be understood;*
> *May I understand.*

Say whatever it is that you need to hear right now. Then set a timer for twenty minutes. Get in a comfortable position, either sitting or lying down, and take three deep breaths. Now place your hand or hands on your heart or another place you find soothing (some people place their hand on their bellies or on their cheeks). You are giving yourself this soothing touch to let your body know you intend to nurture yourself.

Then relax yourself from your head to your feet, sort of like a quick mini body scan. Notice your breathing where you feel it the most. For some people, it is the bottom of their nostrils, where the air going in is a little cooler than the air going out. Some people notice their breath in their chests and others in their bellies. Wherever that is for you, watch your breath go in and out. You are focusing your attention on your breath. Your mind will wander almost immediately, when it does, gently bring your attention back to your breath.

After about five minutes, add your loving kindness phrases for yourself. If this feels strange, start by saying your loving kindness phrases to someone else you pretend is with you. Who is someone that makes you smile? Who is someone with whom your relationship is baggage-free? For Deborah, that might be her best friend, Judy or her cat, Cosmo.

The phrases would start with "May you," instead of "May I." For instance:

May you know that you are loved;
May you be safe;
May you be understood.

39

Really picture the being that you have chosen in your mind's eye. Say the phrases to that image, letting the words sink in to your heart. When your mind wanders, go back to the image of your chosen being and the phrases. Let your heart open.

After about five minutes of this, add yourself to the picture. Now you will be saying, "May we," instead of "May you." Picture the two of you together. Feel the safety and warmth of just being with someone or something that makes you happy. What a relief to be saying the phrases for the two of you. When your mind wanders, gently bring it back to the image of the two of you and repeat your phrases.

May we know that we are loved;
May we be safe;
May we be understood.

After about five minutes, let your friend go and feel the love and compassion pouring down on yourself as you say the phrases to yourself. Continue for about five minutes, bathing yourself in compassion. When you feel the phrases working, your chest might be warm and your heart open. Let that feeling register for a few breaths. You are installing a positive mental state and rewiring your brain.

Then let the phrases go and sit with your eyes closed and notice what comes up. What thoughts, feelings, and emotions are arising? Whatever they are, just let them be; they're not permanent, and they'll come and go. Then gently open your eyes.

Stay connected with friends. Join a support group. Have a glass of wine with someone. Do things with other people that help you feel like you are participating in life—fully. Join a book club, learn a foreign language. Look at the things you have been putting off until 'tomorrow' and do them now.

Know that you are doing all you can in this time of suffering. Know that you are not alone. Know you are loved. Know you are appreciated. Know that this terrible shit does happen and seems so random, but there it is happening when you least expect it. Know that *nothing* is permanent, so these really painful and raw feelings will eventually change to something less harsh. Know that by focusing your attention on a word or phrase, *you can change your relationship to the pain* so that it feels more possible to bear. Know that you are smart and strong and have courage to spare. Know that one day, you will find the silver lining in this mess.

Deborah's best friend, Judy, was indispensable during her trauma. Judy and her husband, Phil, had been pillars of the community, very social and philanthropic. Then, she and her community found out—at the same moment—that Phil had a secret second family. He was hiding a wife and one child. When it became public, on the front page of their local newspaper, the shock and humiliation was unbearable. This happened years before Deborah's personal hurricane. So not only could Judy sympathize with Deborah, but also she could empathize with every bone in Deborah's body.

Lest all you single folk feel left out, infidelity can happen in any relationship that is agreed to be monogamous. So the woman that walks in on her boyfriend with another woman is exactly the same as the married woman in terms of the physical sensations and emotions coming up in her body. All the same tools can be employed to help you feel better, whether you are married or single, young or older. (Although I'm sure the tool you would like to have at that moment is a hammer!)

I was flabbergasted when I learned of a website designed to provide a service for cheaters to hook up with other cheaters. It's called Ashley Madison and its tag line is "Find Your Moment." Ashley Madison claims to have more than 31,545,000 anonymous members! So I guess their claim of being the world's leading dating service for discreet encounters must be true. Their website has a blog, articles, news, and even an affiliate program.

Since Ashley Madison claims to be the world's leading dating site for cheaters, I typed "website for having an affair" into Google and a whole page of lovely garbage popped up. (Yes, I *am* judging here.) One website even ranked the ten best affair sites! These sites are for all people in relationships, not just married people.

Now of course I know plenty of women cheat on their men. Statistics show that women cheat at the same rates as men, but usually for different reasons. Charles J. Orlando, author of the book *The Problem with Women Is...Men,* claims that women cheat for emotional attachment, which means they most likely have already mentally checked out of whatever relationships they're in. Men often cheat for the physical connection, in other words, sex. (Duh!)

In a *Time* magazine article from January 7, 2015, Jeffrey Kluger reported the stereotypes—women cheating for emotional connection and men for physical connection—are true. He cited new research from Chapman University in Orange County, California, that studied the behavior of 63,894 men and women aged 18 to 65. The participants were asked to choose whether they would be hurt more by the "carnal or cuddly" part of someone cheating on them. The men in the study were more upset by the sex part of their partners' cheating. The women in the study were more upset by the perceived emotional connection that their partners might be having with someone else.

The Chapman study showed that both the idea of the sex and the emotional aspect of their partners cheating upset gay or bisexual men and women equally. (One more reason I love gay men!)

The reason I didn't include any sad cheating stories from a man who's been scorned is because I personally don't know of any. In my world, all the injured parties just happen to be women. This next story is about a woman who used the methods of loving kindness meditation to triumph in the face of betrayal and rejection.

NANCY

One of my students, Nancy, found out that her sister Beth had had sex with Nancy's fiancé. After picking herself up and brushing herself off, Nancy did a body scan each and every day for six weeks. She got really comfortable dropping her awareness down into her body and figuring out all the places where she was feeling tightness or pain. She imagined gently placing a warm compress on all her aches. She said it really helped her feel like she was taking control over her body and her emotions. She also reported that it helped the pain and that her body felt so much better and more relaxed after a body scan.

Nancy also used loving kindness meditation phrases every day. She told me she put her hand on her heart and repeated the standard loving kindness phrases: May I be safe; may I be happy; may I be healthy; may I live with ease. She also made up phrases, wrote them down on notecards, and put them on her nightstand, in her bathroom, and on the front of her refrigerator door. She wrote: May I know that I am loved. May I keep an open heart. May I have the courage to forgive. May I have peace in my soul.

Luckily, Nancy has a very warm and loving support network. Our class became a sanctuary for her. One thing about being rejected is that there isn't a soul who hasn't experienced rejection at one time or another, and that sense of shared humanity held her in a warm embrace. Outside of class, Nancy has a great group of friends and co-workers. It showed real courage for her to reach out and connect with people, but once she did, the love poured right in.

Interestingly, Nancy was able to forgive her sister. She kept her heart open just like she prayed she would. Her sister felt true remorse. A series of mitigating circumstances influenced her sister's behavior, and while they didn't excuse the behavior, at least Nancy could feel compassion for her sister instead of anger. She did, however, banish her ex-fiancé from her life. She said she wasn't holding onto anger toward him; she didn't want the toxic emotions in her body. At the same time, she didn't want a person like him in her life. Thank God she learned about him before they got married.

Nancy credits her Mindful Methods practice for getting her through what she says has been the worst experience of her life. She said that, before learning these techniques, if something bad happened in her life, she would "go fetal"—roll up into the fetal position and pull the covers over her head. When she had to get up, she would do something to numb the pain, like drink too much or take pain meds. With the Mindful Methods tools she has now, she feels the most balanced she has in her whole life. That's not surprising because she has the skills to handle whatever unfolds in her future.

LISA: A DIFFERENT FORM OF BETRAYAL

In July of 2013, Lisa experienced an emotional tsunami that knocked her off her feet and shattered the very core of her self-concept. Something was amiss with her credit. She made a few calls and after the bank explained that her credit line was maxed and her mortgage was borrowed against, what unfolded was truly unimaginable. Her brother-in-law told her, "Yes, Larry borrowed 40,000 dollars. He told me not to tell you."

Then, her brother informed her, "Yes, Larry borrowed 60,000 dollars, I promised I wouldn't tell you, he needed it right away so he wouldn't lose his investment in the new business venture in Mexico."

The neighbors, oh, the neighbors. Her husband had borrowed large sums of money from some of the neighbors in their upper middle class New England neighborhood. He forged her name on promissory notes and loan documents. One day the phone rang and her daughter answered the call. A man's voice threatened to beat up her daughter if she didn't pay up—the caller thought it was Lisa answering the phone. This was a genuine nightmare from which she couldn't wake up.

Lisa thought she had known this man, her husband for almost 30 years. She trusted him. He always had her back. That is until 2013, when she was stripped of everything she knew to be her life. He cleaned out their bank accounts. He cleaned out their kids' college funds. He even impersonated her voice and emptied her 401K from work. The police were involved. The FBI was involved. He refused to vacate their home. The facts of this story are so huge and disturbing it is hard to fathom. So the question is, how did she survive?

As you can imagine, Lisa was in tremendous emotional pain and trauma. Everything except her children was taken from her. And it was the thought of abandoning her children that prevented her from taking her own life.

Lisa and Larry lived a noticeably public life. They were active in their community. They gave money to charity. He was president of their church. They had lavish parties and took exotic vacations. They had lots of friends together in their world. Then the curtain fell. This may seem like a champagne problem for someone like this, but imagine everything going to hell. She didn't know whether she would be homeless. She dropped out of society. She had a part-time job as a therapist, and she had a job at a small local college, so she luckily was able to ramp up to working 60 hours or more a week to pay the bills. She lost her community. She was no longer socializing with friends. She had no money to dine out, or go to movies. She worked and went home, then worked and went home. That's what most people in the world do, with a date night or night out budgeted in every so often, but it was a radical change in lifestyle for Lisa.

Lisa is a Mindful Self Compassion teacher, just like me. Thankfully, she had already taken the Mindful Self Compassion course before this fiasco. And she took the teacher training while still in the throes of her emotional turbulence. She said she did a lot of crying and just kept asking herself, "What do I need?" and "What do I need to hear right now?"

She said it was extremely difficult to meditate because of where her mind would go. Any suggestion that eventually she might discover a silver lining was absurd. Trying to manufacture a positive mental state was impossible. What did work was grounding herself with the soles of her feet and listening to guided meditation.

"I was able to go to a place where I'm okay, it's not my fault, and I shouldn't be ashamed."

Lisa says the frustrating part is that she still sometimes wrestles with the unknowable: how this happened and how she didn't see it coming. Those questions have no answer, but she gives herself compassion knowing that *it is human to try to make sense of the senseless.* When I asked whether she is okay now, two years later, she said she is not sure. She gets up every morning, gets dressed and goes to work. When her emotional hurricane hit her, one of her mentors was magnificent in his ability to hold all her pain and suffering. What really has helped, she said, is that she can hold the space for the suffering of others.

Eventually, teaching MSC helped Lisa to heal. She said that teaching these practices to other people gave her the sense of common humanity. "These people are coming to me because they all suffer," she says. "That helped minimize my sense of isolation. And one day a question bubbled up into my consciousness and I heard a voice ask 'Who am I to be different from anyone else?'"

MINDFUL METHODS FOR BEING YOUR OWN BFF (BEST FRIEND FOREVER!)

1. **Body Scan**. Remember that you may feel tingling when you concentrate your attention on each body part, or you may feel nothing. It's okay. Just stick with it. Every time your mind wanders, gently bring your attention back to whatever part of the body you were on before your attention wandered off. If you can't remember where you left off, start over with the toes on your left foot. I used to always fall asleep during a body scan. One time when I was upset, I tried doing a body scan and I stayed awake the whole time and it actually calmed me down. That's when I realized the

beauty of this method. So try it for a number of situations and see whether it works for you like it does for me.

2. **Loving Kindness Phrases.** I say loving kindness phrases for myself all the time. Whenever I feel an emotion coming up that feels bad, my hand automatically goes to my heart, and I wish myself gorgeous things, like safety, peace, ease, love and happiness. Even when I'm not upset, I wish these things for myself. On a shelf in my closet, I keep a wooden figure of a woman made by Kelly Rae Roberts with angel wings on her back and quotes on her flat body. She stands about sixteen inches tall. Every day, I read the quotes out loud first thing in the morning when I am getting dressed:

> "Dear You, may you give yourself permission to trust your voice, step into your power, and know that what you're doing matters."

3. **Stay connected with friends**. This seems like a no-brainer but most of us submerge and dive down like a submarine when we get really sad or depressed. Isolating ourselves only makes depression easier to take hold. I know for myself that when I've been at the bottom

of the snake pit, I really haven't wanted to share my story with friends because I get sick of hearing my own story. I got professional help. I paid a wonderful therapist to hear my story. The Mindful Methods I am teaching in this book are not a substitute for therapy. They are a fabulous addition to therapy. I haven't been depressed for many years now, and I know that it was the combination of medicine, therapy, and my meditation and self-compassion practice that contributed to my healing.

CHAPTER 3

REWIRE YOUR BRAIN

IT'S WILD TO consider it, but what we think can change our brain. Dan Siegel, MD, author of many books on neuroscience and neurobiology, says it simply in his book *Mindsight*: "One of the key practical lessons of modern neuroscience is that the power to direct our attention has within it the power to shape our brain's firing patterns, as well as the power to shape the architecture of the brain itself."

ZOEY

My friend Zoey is a single parent of fraternal twin girls. We met in the mother-of-twins playgroup when the kids were babies. After her divorce, she moved up to the San Francisco area to be closer to her parents. I don't see her much anymore, but we have a strong long-distance friendship. I'm sharing Zoey's parenting stories to illustrate that rewiring one's brain is not only possible, but undeniably beneficial with the right methods and practice. I'm also relaying this story because, frankly, misery loves company!

Zoey's twin girls, Meghan and Michelle, applied to only one college. Actually, Meghan applied for both her and her sister. Meghan gave up her reserved single in the dorm so that she and Michelle could be roommates. That was the only way Michelle would go to college. At the end of the summer, Michelle decided she didn't want to leave home. She was scared. She wasn't ready. To get Meghan to go on her own, Zoey had to agree to buy out Michelle's portion of the room because all the single rooms were assigned, and Meghan was afraid to have a stranger for a roommate. Zoey moved Meghan in and they created a terrific oasis in Meghan's dorm room. Michelle stayed home in Marin County and went to community college. Sounds fine so far, yes? No, definitely not fine.

Zoey was led to believe the daughter away at college, Meghan, was doing well. Every time they spoke on the phone, Meghan told her how happy she was and how much she loved school. Zoey was so proud! She mailed her care packages, rain boots (the school was in Oregon), warm jackets, etc.

Meanwhile, Michelle organized her life around taking the train down the coast of California to visit her boyfriend in Los Angeles on weekends. It was no secret that Michelle was a source of frustration for Zoey. She would go to Los Angeles most weekends and say she would be home on Monday. Monday would become Tuesday. Tuesday would become Wednesday. Wednesday would become Thursday. Her cell phone would be lost, or dead, or God knows where. Her semester at community college started with five courses. That course load decreased to four, then three, and finally two because of missed classes. Her boyfriend was a drug addict who had no interest in helping Michelle be the best she could be. Zoey knew he was a bad influence. But something in Michelle's low self-esteem or shaky identity kept her going back to him. Zoey blamed herself because the girls hadn't grown up with their father, and she thought maybe if they'd had their dad around, things might be more stable now.

One afternoon, while Zoey was having a contentious argument with Michelle's boyfriend, he defended Michelle by saying, "Well, at least she's not as bad as her sister! Michelle would never drop out of school without telling you and cash the tuition refund check like Meghan did!"

Zoey was stunned. She called me absolutely freaking out. She asked several questions I didn't know how to answer.

"This couldn't be true, could it? Could Meghan have dropped out of school? Could she have been lying all this time? And what about the tuition refund check? Is that even possible?"

After she spoke to me, Zoey took a breath and got on the phone with school representatives in the Registrar's

Office, the Admissions Office, and the Housing Office. It was true. Meghan *had* dropped out of school, cashed the $3,800 refund check, and was having a good ol' time shacking up with her boyfriend in a town 30 minutes away from her college.

Zoey had to come up with a plan. Get the kid home. Get the kid in therapy. Once Meghan was home, she asked her what kind of a person could practice such deception. Meghan said she was so ashamed that she was unwilling to discuss the topic with her mother.

"Well, thank God," Zoey said. "That means you have a conscience."

A year later, Zoey reports that Meghan is doing well. She is living at home, going to cosmetology school, and planning on becoming a hairdresser. She said that maybe one day she would like to open her own hair salon. She is still seeing her therapist.

Why is Zoey surviving all this? Zoey, like me, has taken the teachings of Dan Siegel and Rick Hanson to heart and mind, and she has rewired her brain.

Rick Hanson, a neuropsychologist and author of *Buddha's Brain* and *Hardwiring Happiness*, says we can use the mind to change the brain to change the mind for the better. It is the fundamental notion of experience-dependent neuroplasticity: we can change our brain. Our thoughts and emotions fire neurons in our brains, which then wire together and form new neural circuits. What fires together, wires together. Hanson explains in

Hardwiring Happiness, "Taking in the good is the deliberate internalization of positive experiences in implicit memory."

Hanson explains that our brain, unless it learns to do otherwise, tends to hang on to negative experiences like Velcro, while positive experiences can feel like they slip off Teflon. Valid evolutionary reasons exist for this. As we all know, our ancestors needed the fight/flight/freeze response to survive. They were looking for dangers and ruminating on past mistakes to stay safe. This happens in the brain region called the amygdala, which acts instantly, and is thought to come from our reptilian phase of evolution. So how do we install good experiences in long-term memory so they will stick? And how do you know which experiences will be the most helpful to your unique personality?

Rick Hanson explains that you first need to diagnose what is ailing you to be able to choose the best category of things to take in and install in your brain. Then, you need to give the transitioned good mental state time to install in your brain in order to turn it into a positive neural trait that can last.

So make sure to really feel a good mental state for a couple of breaths. Not "that's a beautiful sunset, what's for dinner" but rather, "that's a beautiful sunset. Wow, look at those colors. It's really gorgeous. I'm so happy to have this moment." Make it as intense a feeling for as long as you can to ensure that it becomes a positive neural trait. What follows is a method that will help you with this:

H.E.A.L. METHOD

Hanson devised an anagram to help us remember how to turn good experiences into brain changers: **H.E.A.L.**

H = Have a good experience.

E = Enrich it to install it.

A = Absorb it as if you are filling your body up with the good feeling of the experience.

L = Link positive and negative material. This is an optional last step, which explains how to link the positive experience with a memory of a negative experience to try to supplant the bad with the good.

Have the good experience and enjoy it!

When I first started learning this, I would find myself looking at the sunset and saying to myself, *breathe it in; really feel it; it's gorgeous.* That was enough time for me to install that particular good experience into my brain.

One day, my husband and I were walking our dogs at this terrific dog park in San Diego called Fiesta Island. The sun was shining, the wind blowing lightly, the bay absolutely beautiful, and all around us were happy dogs roaming everywhere we looked. My husband said something about it being terrific, and I couldn't resist but to smile and say, "Let it fill you up, really take in the good feeling. You are rewiring your brain!"

After making a daily practice of taking in the good for a couple of years, I can tell you I have rewired my brain. People may think it's strange when I say that, but there is no question that I am a happier, more resilient person than I was five years ago. You don't need to use the anagram in order to remember to take in a good mental state. Whenever you have a great feeling, take it in for a few breaths.

I know I'm more resilient because I can take an emotional hit and get up faster than I used to. The day-to-day disappointments and frustrations that we all experience used to really stick in my mind and surface into my consciousness over and over. That no longer happens.

I can be frustrated or disappointed, and the event falls out of my head. I can call it up, of course. It's not like I've forgotten what happened. It's just that it isn't haunting my thoughts. I'm not ruminating like I used to. And I'm not worrying about the future as much.

One of my students, who is a grandmother, loves it when her daughter calls and puts her baby on FaceTime to talk to Grandma. She has learned to pull up that memory into her consciousness to give herself that positive mental state every day.

Zoey too can handle all the craziness and disappointment because she doesn't ruminate on it. Like me, she has positive experiences constantly firing and rewiring in her brain. Sure, she feels the shock, the horror, disappointments and frustrations but it doesn't take her down like before. She now deals with it. She is proactive. She is standing in a shit storm with a fabulous umbrella. And you can have that wonderful umbrella at any age!

You are never too old to rewire your brain for more happiness and resilience. There is a fabulous YouTube video seen by more than 300,000 people called *Confessions of a Jewish Mother: How My Son Ruined My Life*. Selma Baraz, the late mother of James Baraz, of *Awakening Joy* fame, recounts how much she used to love to complain and worry, and how when her son was visiting, he got so sick of all her negativity that he taught her a gratitude practice that caused her to eventually rewire her brain for more happiness. The video is hysterical because she is already in her nineties, and her delivery and timing are just perfect. She really loved her life of kvetching, and I honestly think she was shocked that she could let that all go. But let it go she did, and her last few years were more serene! How wonderful to figure that out, even late in life.

MINDFUL METHODS YOU CAN USE TO REWIRE YOUR BRAIN

H.E.A.L. Rewire your brain!

1. H=Have a good experience.
   Diagnose what is ailing you to choose the best category of things to take in and install in your brain.

2. E=Enrich it to install it.
   Give the good mental state time to install in your brain in order to turn it into a positive neural trait. Really feel it for a couple of breaths.

3. A=Absorb it
   Enjoy filling your body up with the good feeling of the experience. Make it as intense a feeling for as long as you can.

4. L=Link
   This is an optional last step that explains how to link the positive experience with a memory of a negative experience to try to supplant the bad with the good. Have the good experience and enjoy!

How to do H.E.A.L. depending on your needs right now:

If you're feeling lonely, resentful, and hurt, you should take in experiences where you feel appreciated and provide you with a sense of belonging. Hanson explains that feeling left out and hurt means that your need to attach to others is not being met. He calls this the "attaching to others system." Just remembering times when you were hanging out with a friend or even cuddling up with your pet can help you feel attached.

If you feel worried and helpless, then your need for safety is not being met, or as Hanson puts it, your needs are falling into the "avoiding harms system." In that case, install experiences where you feel safe, strong, and relaxed. When I felt disappointment, sadness, and frustration at my kids or at myself because of my parenting, I installed experiences where I felt a sense of gratitude, pleasure, accomplishment, and satisfaction. The compassionate letter exercises and maintaining a daily gratitude practice that I explain in Chapter 5 validate this approach.

The Guest House
Rumi

This being human is a guest house.
Every morning a new arrival.

A joy, a depression, a meanness,
some momentary awareness comes
as an unexpected visitor.

Welcome and entertain them all!
Even if they're a crowd of sorrows,
who violently sweep your house
empty of its furniture,
still, treat each guest honorably.

He may be clearing you out
for some new delight.

The dark thought, the shame, the malice,
meet them at the door laughing,
and invite them in.

Be grateful for whoever comes,
because each has been sent
as a guide from beyond.

CHAPTER 4

LET YOUR HEART RADIATE WITH LOVE: BUST YOUR BRA MOMENTS

FEELING SAFE IS a basic human requirement. You need to feel safe in the world, in your family, your community, your work. At its root, feeling safe means feeling safe being in your skin, in being alive, in being you.

One way of creating that sense of protection–even when life feels very treacherous—is through Soothing Touch and Loving Kindness Meditation.

SOOTHING TOUCH

When a child is hurt, a caring adult can reach out with a soothing touch and a soft voice to comfort the child. That soothing touch and gentle voice taps into the mammalian caregiver response and produces the release of oxytocin and opiates in both adults and children. What I have found in my work with many people is that many don't realize they can give themselves that same act of nurturing. Here's how:

Place your hand on your own body with the intention of soothing yourself whenever you feel bad. By doing that simple act you tap into *your* mammalian caregiver response and your body releases soothing oxytocin and opiates. The release of those calming hormones counteracts the cortisol and adrenaline that are released into your brain during stressful moments. Cortisol and adrenaline get released whenever you have a fight/flight/freeze response to an actual or perceived danger. Its important to remember that the scared, fearful feeling you are experiencing is a natural response, just as bleeding is a response when you are injured. It's there to protect you.

Whenever you have a negative emotion, it also activates your fight/flight/freeze response. If you then beat yourself up or become self-critical for having the negative emotion—*I screwed up, I always screw everything up*—you add a second poison arrow, making the reaction you feel even worse.

To get yourself back in control over that ruminating cycle and regulate your system in a positive way, try Soothing Touch. It's easy and effective no matter what is happening in your life.

HAND ON HEART

Put your hand or hands on your heart. If the heart isn't or hasn't been your soothing place, try your belly, your face, or your arms. Place your hands on your body where you feel your hands relax and your body feels soothed. You will begin to feel calm, but only if your intent is genuine. This is not about faking a cure. This is about having a true connection between your mind, your body and your emotions.

This can be is a remarkably powerful gesture for you with instantaneous results of self-nurturance. If you don't feel it right away, wait, count to ten and do it again.

LOVING KINDNESS MEDITATION

Loving Kindness Meditation is an English translation of the Pali word *metta*. Pali was the language in the time of the Buddha, 2,500 years ago. *Metta* means love, friendliness, benevolence, and goodwill. *Metta* meditation teaches us how to be better friends to ourselves. An often-cited, famous study done by Barbara Fredrickson at the University of North Carolina in 2008 compared people who had done seven weeks of Loving Kindness Meditation with a control group of people on her waiting list. Her testing proved that Metta meditation significantly increased positive emotions such as love, joy, gratitude, hope, and awe in everyone who learned how to do it. It also increased problem-solving ability, physical health, mindfulness, self-acceptance, positive relations with others, and savoring the future. That double-blind test sold it for me!

Soothing Touch and Loving Kindness Meditation are used in many different situations. You can apply these methods whenever you need them to soothe yourself. They may prompt a warm expansive feeling in your chest, almost as if you might "bust your bra."

In the following story, you can see how I used Loving Kindness phrases, my here-and-now stone, a gratitude practice, and a body-scan meditation to help me get through a very scary and frightening time.

It was October 23, 2012, at around 8:15 a.m., when my daughter Cara, then seventeen years old, had a terrible car accident. She was driving a different route to school because one of her friends, who had spent the night at our house, needed to stop home for her backpack. As she crested the little incline of the exit ramp, she noticed cars backed up below her but didn't have time to stop and rear-ended the car in front of her. Before the ambulance came, she called her dad, my husband, Lowell, and said, "Dad, I've been in an accident; I'm hurt." He told her not to move, identified her exact location, and jumped in the car to find her. At the time I was in Massachusetts at a six-day retreat with the Institute for Jewish Spirituality. Lowell called and told me to stay near my phone. It was the first day of the retreat. I immediately arranged for a flight home.

Lowell arrived at the crash site to find the ambulance already gone. The police said they had no idea what hospital Cara was taken to. He began to call all the hospitals in the area but his search proved fruitless. He began to repeat the calls and discovered that she was in the Emergency Room at UCSD, a hospital in Hillcrest, a downtown neighborhood of San Diego only twenty minutes away. As it turned out it was the same hospital where she and her twin sister, Danielle were born. We knew it well eighteen years ago. Lowell called me, relieved that he had found her, but concerned that he no longer knew anyone on staff there who could help us coordinate all her care at UCSD.

However, as a coincidence, the week before I was at a theatrical performance in Hillcrest and I ran into Dr. Moore, the perinatologist who delivered our twins and who took care of me. It was a wonderful and warm encounter, with lots of hugs and catching up. This was the doctor who had saved my life!

I told my husband to hang on and that I would get through to Dr. Moore's office. Dr. Moore's assistant got through to him and within the hour, Cara had the "A" trauma team, and Lowell had tender loving care from Dr. Moore's department. A fabulous nursing director kept checking on both Lowell and Cara's twin sister Danielle, once she arrived. Without that personal touch and care, this already traumatic experience would have been so much worse for them.

On the flight home I practiced Mindful Methods to keep myself together. I knew I wasn't freaking out because I was using a mantra, focusing my mind over and over on the word "safe." I also focused my attention on my breath for a few minutes every hour or so. I remember spending a lot of time talking with the flight attendants, who were very sympathetic. I didn't know the results or the prognosis until I landed, so I had to live for five and a half hours in the space of not knowing, a tough place to be in when it comes to the safety of your child.

Cara fractured five vertebrae in her back. She was lucky to be alive. She was lucky to be able to walk. We took Cara home from the hospital in a body brace. She was in excruciating pain. Dr. Moore referred us to a well-known back surgeon, who admitted Cara right away as a new patient. He said that she was experiencing so much pain because her brace was not adequate. She had injuries that were outside of the range of the MRI that was done at the hospital she had been admitted to after the accident.

The orthopedic surgeon's team built her a custom brace, a plastic shell that was created after a plaster cast was molded onto her body. She also had a neck piece screwed to the shell to hold her neck and head in one place. She had to wear this at all times—24 hours a day. The slightest wrong touch or misstep could bring back the searing pain. So showering looked like this: she would walk into the shower in her brace and sit down on a stool. I would carefully take her brace off, slowly take her t-shirt off, soap her up and rinse off, dry her off still seated, put her t-shirt back on, put her brace on, have her stand up, dry the rest of the way off, and then we'd step out of the shower. It was tense!

This was a scary time for everyone in our family. I slept on a cot in Cara's room in our home for months. She needed the room so cold (because the body cast was warm) that I slept with a hat, gloves, scarf and leggings under my pajamas! It was important for me to administer her medicine on a timely basis so we could keep ahead of the pain. I was so worried about prescription drug addiction that, after a month, I allowed her to use a marijuana derivative, CBD, which is a painkiller that doesn't make you high. I also allowed some THC use, which made me very uncomfortable even though it was legal and prescribed. Luckily, I had a lot of help then, through my parents, husband and others.

The techniques that Cara and I used during her convalescence are the techniques I learned during the eight week Mindful Self-Compassion (MSC) course that I took in 2011, and some techniques from the Awakening Joy course, the gratitude practice, that I had taken the year before. The techniques recalibrated Cara. She became a different person. For me, these methods worked gorgeously, allowing me to move from a space of fear and frustration to grace and gratitude.

MINDFUL METHODS FOR FEELING SAFE

1. **Loving Kindness Phrases**
   Loving kindness phrases are wishes. Traditional phrases include:

   > May I be safe.
   > May I be happy.
   > May I be healthy.
   > May I live with ease.

   For people who don't feel those phrases work for them, they create their own for their own unique situation. You can too. I like the idea of creating your own Loving Kindness phrases. What phrases you would like to hear every day for the rest of your life? Think about what you need to hear. The needs I'm talk are universal human needs—core needs that would cause you suffering if they were not met. Some examples of universal core needs are safety, stability, love, connection, trust, authenticity, peace, ease, and harmony.

   Write down the phrases that would fill you with gratitude whenever you hear them and practice focusing your attention during meditation on those phrases. If you need to hear "I love you" every day and you want to morph that into a loving kindness phrase for yourself, it might sound something like this; "May I know I am loved." Or "May I love myself just as I am."

My students create Loving Kindness phrases for a ritual we participate in during my course. Each person reads a wish for himself or herself, followed by a wish for the world. Maybe one of their phrases will resonate with you! If you connect with one of these phrases and it would make you happy to hear it every day, copy that phrase for yourself.

I am loved.
You are loved.

May I feel safe and live with ease.
May you feel safe and happy.

May I have patience.
May you be truly happy.

May I be the best version of myself.
May you feel good about being your authentic self.

May I be safe.
May you be healthy.

May I experience self-compassion.
May you always live with ease instead of dis-ease.

May I be loved and appreciated.
May I be valued.
May I be kind.
May you be loved, appreciated, valued and kind.
May the world be filled with gratitude for the life we share.

May I accept myself fully, not take things personally, and may I continue my attitude of gratitude.
May the world be at peace and all feel kindness and compassion toward each other.

May I be a blessing.
May you feel safe and have a meaningful life.

May I know peace so that I can see it in others as well.
May all beings be happy and know peace—no exceptions!

May I forgive myself.
May you tolerate those who are unlike you.

My I love my life
May you get comfortable living in the moment and not reacting from fear.

May I feel that what I'm doing has value.

May you and all beings realize you and they contribute to the success of mankind.

During Cara's convalescence, I repeated Loving Kindness phrases to myself many times a day. "May we be safe; may we be happy; may we be healthy; may we live with ease." I also repeated the phrase, "Whatever unfolds, I will be there to meet it." And I made specific phrases that I said to myself just for Cara. "May you heal completely; may you be free of pain; may you be free of addiction."

There was tons of downtime while I sat in the rocking chair in her room. At times I went into such deep meditative states that I was unsure whether I was asleep or awake. I created all kinds of healing and nurturing phrases for myself during that time. It was pretty awful, and meditating with Loving Kindness phrases took my anxiety way down. The days I walked Cara from her room to the car to drive her to a doctor appointment, I could feel my nerves shoot through the roof. She was so traumatized by her accident that she was petrified of another car accident. She would gasp and act like a backseat driver from the front seat. I would have really felt like a basket case if I didn't have something to ground me. I knew I had to ground myself to not allow myself to feel Cara's fear. I breathed, sometimes put my hand on my heart, and talked to myself in my head, telling myself everything was going to be all right. We made it to the doctor and home again without a hitch.

2. Here-and-Now Stone

It became obvious that I had to find a way to give Cara the same source of peacefulness and confidence about her healing. But, teaching your own daughter what you know, is like trying to teach her how to drive a car.

So I invited a highly recommended healing touch practitioner to come to the house to do energy work with Cara, primarily to help her to heal. She moved her hands above Cara's body, not touching her but moving the air above her, as if to affect Cara's energy fields. I am not qualified to explain the theory behind this modality, but I knew that there had been anecdotal evidence that the woman had helped others. It couldn't hurt Cara to try it, right?

The healer had a soft soothing voice and manner. She gave Cara a beautiful red polished stone shaped like a heart. It became a stone that Cara used to focus her attention on if she felt pain or anxiety. That helped Cara feel and look more peaceful and relaxed than I had seen in a long time. I'm glad that we had the visit from the healing touch practitioner. We'll never know if it helped the nature of Cara's recovery, but it provided a lovely interlude in an otherwise difficult recovery.

3. **Gratitude Practice.**

   If you keep a notebook or journal, you might want to write down four things you are grateful for each day. Or, if you are like me and you don't enjoy journaling, answer two questions in your journal or on a notebook you can keep near you every night:

   1. What are you grateful for today?
   2. What did you enjoy today?

You can write one word answers, or whole paragraphs. Example:

   I. I am grateful about my conversation with Sylvie. Or,
   II. My daughter, Sylvie called me today. I listened to her talk about her new job and boyfriend. I didn't talk about me for a change. Instead I focused completely on her, listened to her. She's a beautiful,

compassionate child and I told her that. She seemed surprised I was so curious about her, what she was doing and news about her friends.

III. Today I enjoyed peace and quiet.

IV. It was great having my daughter Josie and her husband and the kids visit me for a week. Even though I miss them, it was nice today to be able to garden and plant the small rosemary bush I bought at the street fair on Sunday.

Your ideas don't need to be monumental. They could be as simple as gratitude for having some good friends in your life or clean sheets on your bed. When possible, write longhand instead of typing on a device. As you probably know by now, many experts believe that the physical act of writing has more benefits to your right brain, the creative side of your brain than typing on a keyboard.

When you feel creative it lifts your spirit. Remember that whether you write longhand or type, you still get all the health and wellness benefits of keeping a journal dedicated to your gratitude practice.

Lower blood pressure and a stronger immune system are your initial health benefits from a Gratitude Practice. Others are higher levels of positive emotions, such as joy, optimism and happiness; more compassion and generosity, both in giving and receiving; and the feeling of being less lonely and isolated. The benefits of gratitude practice have been written about extensively. Robert Emmons, a professor in UC Davis' psychology department and author of *Gratitude Works*, says that once you've embraced gratitude, give it around three weeks before you and others see changes in your behavior.

It takes that long for a behavior to become a habit. You want your changes to become permanent, right? So, as your brain re-wires, you automatically feel the change too. What could be easier?

I subscribe to a wonderful newsletter from the Greater Good Science Center out of University of California, Berkeley. I recommend subscribing to their newsletter to read about their comprehensive three-year study on gratitude. My hope is that their findings will encourage all of us to make a gratitude practice part of our lives at home and at work. They already have dozens of articles discussing how gratitude practices can improve our happiness and well-being.

Reading their articles is a great reminder to keep up your practice, whether it is a gratitude practice, or one of the many mindfulness, meditation, and compassion practices that they frequently present and review. Their website and newsletter are listed in the resources section at the end of this book. I hope you enjoy reading their posts as much as I have.

During the months of Cara's convalescence, I kept an all-encompassing gratitude practice going. She and I talked every single day about how grateful we were that she was alive and that she wouldn't be in a wheelchair for the rest of her life. And I was grateful that I had the time to take care of her.

Cara imagined that it was her karma that caused her accident. In retrospect, she thought she was traveling down the wrong path, spiritually speaking. The accident forced her to slow down and reexamine her life. She's found her passion in the healing world, studying to be a master clinical herbalist in addition to her music career as a singer songwriter. The accident was terrible, but we are blessed that the silver lining of the story can be found in the woman Cara is today. Silver lining stories happen all the time, but sometimes it's not until years later that the silver lining is revealed.

For me, it turned out to be a special time when I created an amazing array of healing and nurturing phrases for Cara and myself. And it was the source of a bond between us that has never broken. That silver lining story is continuing to unfold.

4. **Body Scan.**

   This is a powerful Mindful Method for feeling safe. When I was taking care of Cara, I huddled up on my little cot in her room, bundled in layers, trying to relax to go to sleep—and I used the body scan I learned in MBSR. I warmed up by giving attention and a little love to each body part. By the time I got to my torso, I was usually asleep. Cara was usually asleep long before me. It was difficult for me to see her body in that big clamshell of a brace, with her head held in place by a neck piece that was screwed into her chest and the back of the clamshell by metal rods. The saving grace was that the pain meds made her drowsy. Otherwise, I know it would have been extremely difficult for her to sleep in that contraption. The body scan took my mind from how bad I felt for Cara, and changed the focus of my attention. It was impossible to wallow in sadness and worry and fear for her and at the same time practice the body scan. This allowed me to change the channel of my thoughts and concerns long enough to fall asleep.

Thank God there is a happy ending to this story. Cara spent her senior year of high school at home in a body brace with a tutor, but she graduated from high school. Senior year was supposed to be much more fun for her, but she lived through it, made the best of it, and learned so much from her suffering that it changed the direction of her life. Now her goal is to help others who are suffering.

She was able to witness a side of medicine, healing and patience that very few other life situations would have provided her. Who knows whether she would have chosen that path but for the accident? She is a beautiful and spiritual soul who will now impact the lives of everyone she encounters. She is a living message of hope to her family and everyone who knows her. Her personal growth was yet another silver lining that I didn't see coming.

MINDFUL METHODS TO RADIATE SO MUCH LOVE IN YOUR HEART THAT YOU FEEL AS THOUGH YOU MIGHT BUST YOUR BRA TO STAY CALM AMID CHAOS

1. **Loving Kindness Phrases to focus your attention during meditation.** You can start now by trying on all the different loving kindness phrases from this chapter. Say each one and genuinely mean it. Then see how you feel. If you get a warm, expansive, and open-hearted feeling from one of the phrases, write it

down and practice saying it a few times a day. If it keeps giving you that warm feeling in your chest, it's a keeper for you! Make up your own phrases for whatever situation you have going on in your life.

(I watched a short video from Spirit Rock Meditation Center where the teacher recommended silently saying Loving Kindness phrases to strangers who happen to be in line in front of you at the grocery store. The video promised I'd have a different experience waiting in line. I tried it and it's true! It makes waiting in line a pleasant, in the moment, observing experience!)

2. **Here-and-Now Stone**. At this point, I hope I don't have to tell you why you should find a stone and use it! Just do it. It keeps you pleasantly focused on the present.

3. **Gratitude Practice—Write it down!** This is really a huge deal. The science validating this practice is overwhelming. Back in the 1960s, the father of positive psychology, Martin Seligman, did a study that showed that people who kept a gratitude journal had more feelings of well-being even six months after they stopped writing their journals.

The research I provided in this chapter has been newly tested, and the methodologies for getting the statistics are new, authentic and have been verified. The results prove the same old fact: Writing down what you are grateful for each day can make you a happier person. This is one of those times when you can trust forty years of research and millions of other people before you (and me). Do what they've shared with us and enjoy the results!

4. **Body Scan**. This is a meditation practice, not a relaxation practice, but it usually has the side effect of being very relaxing.

One caveat: If you have been physically abused, please do not do a body scan without a therapist or mental health professional in the room to guide you. It is possible for you to get to a part of the body that was the location of the past abuse or trauma and have an adverse emotional reaction that may be too intense for you to handle alone.

CHAPTER 5

YOUR INNER CRITIC:
THANK YOUR INNER BITCH

WE'VE ALL GOT those voices in our heads that speak to us in not the nicest of tones. Those voices are our inner critics. They try to keep us safe, but often not in the best of ways. These are usually the internalized voices of our primary caregivers from our early childhoods. If you were abused and neglected as a child, and the caregiver who was the source of your abuse is the critical voice you hear, this exercise might be too intense and upsetting to be of any value. It comes as no surprise that little kids need to connect to such a person in order to stay alive, to be fed and clothed, even if that person is hurting them. In this case, this voice might even be a hindrance to healing, so if you were greatly abused or neglected as a child, I would suggest skipping the two writing exercises in this chapter that deal with the inner critic.

Chris Germer and Kristin Neff offer a course on the inner critic in their Mindful Self-Compassion curriculum. The concepts are based on Internal Family Systems (IFS) therapy created by Dr. Richard C. Schwartz, and the work of Paul Gilbert, author of *The Compassionate Mind*, who created Compassion Focused Therapy (CFT) for therapists to use with their clients.

Internal Family Systems is a model used by therapists to help their clients heal. IFS was created by Dr. Richard C. Schwartz, a family therapist who realized that the key to helping some of his clients attain wholeness was to deal with the sum of their parts. He created an institution to train clinicians in this model. He now runs conferences and has written many books on this topic. His latest book, *You are the One You've Been Waiting For*, is a fabulous addition to his important body of work. In 2010, Dr. Schwartz endorsed a book for laypeople written by Jay Earley and Bonnie Weiss called *Self-Therapy for Your Inner Critic: Transforming Self-Criticism into Self-Confidence*. He applauded Earley and Weiss for creating a manual that everyday people can use to heal themselves.

I didn't know anything about IFS when I took the eight-week Mindful Self-Compassion course. I understood that the gist was to be curious about what might be driving this inner critic. Does the critic want to motivate me to be my best? Keep me safe? Can you figure out whose voice it is? Is it helpful? And how are we to get in touch with this bitch? You will soon understand why these questions and the possible answers will be helpful as you perform the following exercises.

YOUR INNER-BITCH WRITING EXERCISE

1. Get a pen and paper or your computer or tablet—something you can write with. Pick a behavior you would like to change. Something possible, such as "I eat too much" or "I don't exercise enough" —not "My ears are too big." Now write what your inner bitch, or critic, is saying about this behavior. Pay attention to the tone, not only the words. Write how the tone and the overall way the text is written makes you feel. Is your inner critic kind and respectful? Does the critic teach you in a meaningful way that change would be for your own good? Does the voice inspire you to change?

   To give you an example, I'm going to take you through the exercise so you understand.

   I picked a behavior that I seriously would like to change: I don't exercise enough. It would be healthy to exercise more, and I would feel great if exercise was a regular routine with me instead of something that seemed like an effort. There have been decades where I have exercised regularly, followed by years of sloth, and then decades back on the exercise wagon. Right now, I'm in the sloth tar pit.

My inner critic is saying, "Get up off your ass, woman! The aches and pains you have in your feet DO NOT GIVE YOU AN EXCUSE TO BE A LAZY FAT ASS." So, now I consider if that's nice. No, absolutely not. And what was the tone of voice of that critic? Well, by the all caps, we can tell it was harsh. And how does that make me feel? And this is the biggie here: Does this motivate me to go to the gym? The answer is a resounding NO! The whole thing makes me feel tired, negative, a little less worthy as a person, like no reasonable solution is feasible other than curling up in bed with the covers pulled up under my chin.

2. Now write to yourself from your compassionate voice. Trust me, it's in there. It's the voice that you use when you are comforting a dear friend.

In the case of my example, what if the critic said this instead: "It's okay, honey. At least you are keeping your calories down. I know your feet really do hurt, and I think you are right to keep putting off another foot surgery. Just exercise when you can. It doesn't need to be rigidly three times a week or five times a week. Start small and pat yourself on the back for any time spent exercising. I'd like you to change this behavior and exercise more because I love you and I know it will make you happy to improve your health."

3. Ask yourself how that makes you feel? Wow, that's so much better! I might actually try to get to that yoga class if I talk to myself with the loving tone I would use with a dear friend. Wait a minute! I *am* that dear friend! I can always motivate myself with love instead of criticism. If we spoke to ourselves with care and positive reinforcement, that could make initiating and continuing to work on the desired change more likely.

4. It's time to say thank you and good-bye to that harsh voice inside your head. Ah, inner critic, you've been around for as long as I can remember. I do believe you served me well at times. I certainly tried to get good grades, so thank you. I kept my options open, so thank you. But I was a little stressed out at times, so that didn't always help. I do admit I was over-exercising and under eating in law school, so no thank you. I tried to be the best mom I could be, so thank you. I beat myself up mercilessly for millions of perceived infractions when my unrealistic expectations were not met, so no thank you. And I believe you pushed me to create those unrealistic expectations, so no thank you.

I'll take it from here, inner critic. You can stand down. You've put in too many years of service already.

COMPASSIONATE LETTER TO MYSELF

This exercise was a doozy for me. The instruction is to write a letter to yourself about an issue that is really troubling you from the perspective of an all-knowing, all-loving being. This person or being knows everything about you, including every skeleton in your closet, and yet he or she loves you unconditionally. This entity also knows every good deed you have ever done and has seen every random act of loving kindness you have ever performed.

I remember writing that letter when I took the Mindful Self-Compassion eight-week course in 2011. It was a huge *a-ha* moment. I took it into my therapist appointment, and she actually became emotional.

"Did you really say all those nice things about yourself? Are you sure no one helped you?"

No one helped me. I got in touch with my compassionate voice, and thank God that voice is still with me today.

I'm sharing this letter with you. It was from a time when I was the most vulnerable, the most raw. This exercise was a turning point in my healing:

"I feel inadequate because I gave up my profession in order to be a full-time mother and my kids aren't turning out so wonderfully. So that means, deep down, I feel like a failure. The disappointment in the choices they (twins) are making during their adolescence is crushing. Sometimes it makes me feel depressed and hopeless. Other times I feel angry. I think if I had a job while they were growing up, they would be more self-reliant, and maybe they would be more motivated workers.

I feel envious of the families whose kids get good grades in good schools, and do community service because they want to, and study for the SAT because they know it makes a difference. I'm jealous of the families whose kids love camp, and go away year after year in the summer and then become CITs and counselors. I'm guilty that I have raised kids who feel entitled and behave as though they think the rules don't apply to them and demonstrate little motivation to better themselves."

This is the compassionate response from my imaginary friend:

"Julie, you are not a failure. You gave up your profession because you were lucky enough to have the choice to be there 24/7 for your kids. At the time, you loved that choice. You were an incredibly caring, loving, creative, intelligent mom—in fact, you still are.

Your daughters are still growing and changing. The jury is merely still out on how they will develop as women. They are smart and talented individuals. They just act immature. I'm sure that with your loving and firm guidance they will eventually grow out of their challenging adolescent phase.

You and your husband are doing an admirable job keeping your relationship together while raising two very difficult children.

And as for you, it's not as if you stayed home eating bonbons all these years. Look at all the positive impact you have had on so many organizations. Just think about all the people whom you have helped at the JCC—not only the staff, by implementing and raising the funds for a great retirement plan for them, but also all the people that the JCC serves every day that benefit from the long-term staff. And you were the one that made Shalom Baby a priority and achieved funding to protect that program now and in the future. There are hundreds and hundreds of moms that come together as a community in playgroups, classes and activities because of getting the start at one of the Shalom Baby programs.

And don't forget the Pardes Institute of Jewish Studies in Jerusalem. They wouldn't have an executive seminar if not for you. It was your idea for them to teach a weeklong unit of torah text study and travel in Jerusalem to grown-ups in order to connect them to Pardes. That program has continued successfully for the last eighteen years and still makes a huge difference in donor cultivation. Julie, if you want to do something different with your life, you can do it. You are only fifty-one. The girls will be off to college in a year and a half. You are smart. People love you. They love your honesty. They love your sense of humor. They love that you connect so easily.

What would make you happy? I think it would be useful for you to find something you feel passionate about and where you feel like you add value.

I'm proud of you for taking the time to try to ground yourself by taking meditation classes and practicing yoga and meditation. The spirituality program you are taking is a valuable education. Who knows where that will lead? Yet, in the meantime you are feeling good about yourself and that's important!

Please also know that you are a wonderful mother, wife, daughter, sister, and friend."

I thank everyone who had a hand in creating that exercise and showing me the way to a better life. And at the time of writing that letter, I had no idea I would become a Mindful Self-Compassion teacher. They didn't even begin training people to teach that class until three years later. I love my life now. I adore teaching and am so jazzed when a student asks a question, and I can create an answer from the teachings of so many different scholars, all synthesized in my head.

One of my students generously shared her compassionate letter exercise for this book to offer another perspective.

11/24/14

Issue: I feel tired and unmotivated and then feel inadequate.

I compare myself to others who are more "successful" and making larger contributions in the world and I then feel less than and that I've not done enough nor doing enough and that I haven't maximized my potential in my life. I end up feeling down on myself and ashamed, that I am not worth much. I also get scared that perhaps I am seriously sick and will die soon.

Here is the response from the voice of compassion.

Precious One, you are exactly where you need to be, where we have called you to be. You have had an extraordinary human life and have kept your heart open. We are so very proud of you. You have walked through a very rich but also challenging lifetime and it is your presence, the essence of your Spirit, that makes the difference here, not what you "do".

Your inquiry is so delightfully rich. You just cannot get enough of "living and learning" about the human experience, and you are precious for that. You are also incredibly responsible and take your life seriously, which is beautiful and ethical, which you are.

However, we are calling you now to slow down and rest. We've provided the means for you to do so. You are safe. It's okay. You and those you love will have enough. You are well provided for. Rest. Slow down. Nothing is more important now than that.

We also want you to take that incredibly responsible spirit and turn it toward yourself and your body-temple. Rest. For the next chapter in your life, we need you to have a healthy and stable body to reside in. Nothing is more important.

Create beauty around yourself, for that impacts you greatly. Create spacious light energy around you and let it emanate from your heart. That will impact others more than any technique that you have learned, and you will be able to rest inside of it.

Nourish calmness and inner peace from your heart center. Write.

It is, as you are experiencing right now, a means to access your deeper knowing. FEEL it, expand it. THIS is what heals. THIS is what this precious planet that you love so much needs.

Follow your heart. Trust your inner guidance from your neck down. Remember all that you have learned from direct experience.

Surround yourself with nourishing people for the next year. This is not a time to push through anything nor force anything. Let things flow and they will be effortless and hopefully even fun.

We cherish you and stand fully behind you cheering you on.

It is not your time yet to leave this body, and will not be time for quite awhile. You are not nearly done here yet, so relax, rest up, and enjoy. We are always with you."

How fabulous to soothe yourself in this manner. When you allow yourself to take in and feel a positive mental state in your body, you are rewiring your brain for more happiness and resilience. That is the beauty of experience- dependent neuroplasticity. What you think, changes your brain. If you talk to yourself with gentleness and compassion and you take a couple of moments to savor the good feelings your compassionate voice brings up in you, that positive mental state rewires your brain. Just as when you are filled with a feeling of gratitude or joy, if you let the feeling fill you up for a breath or two, you are rewiring your brain. It is such a simple practice to have profound results! With these two ex-amples, I hope you will be motivated to try this exercise yourself.

MINDFUL METHODS FOR THANKING YOUR INNER BITCH

1. **Compassionate letter about a behavior you would like to change.** Remember to pick a behavior that isn't a doozy, and one that it is possible to change (not "I'm too short"). You should practice choosing different behaviors and writing a letter for each. We all have be-haviors we would like to change. That's why people make New Year's resolutions each year! Imagine if you heard your compassion-ate voice cheering you on? How would that change your motivation?

2. **Compassionate letter about a BIG ISSUE that is troubling you.** Here is where you pick a doozy of an issue. Something that is a huge stumbling block to your happiness. It could be an issue in your interpersonal relationships at home or at work, or it could be a bigger more universal or existential problem. Whatever it is, try to get to the bottom of it. What's un-derneath the pain? Is it fear? What is the fear about? Is it fear of being unlovable? Is it fear of

being unworthy? Is it fear of not being seen, or heard, or loved?

These are universal human needs; we all have them. They're part of being a human being. If we can remember that every single person on earth has these same needs, we will realize we are not alone. That is so powerful. Next time you feel bad because one of your universal human needs is not being met, think about how many billions of people are probably feeling the same thing or worse at the same time! That sense of common humanity not only gives us perspective, but also it helps prevent the sense of isolation that can foster depression.

CHAPTER 6

CHECK YOUR COMPASS: WHAT DIRECTION ARE YOU FACING?

HAVE YOU EVER really thought about your core values? I don't mean goals, like finishing a degree program. I mean values, the things that give your life meaning. If the goal would be to graduate college, the core value would be learning. Goals are a destination; core values are a direction. We need to know what our core values are in order to give ourselves a course correction when we veer off track. Sometimes, the anxiety and frustration we feel stems from the fact that we are not living in accordance with our core values.

Everyone will have some differences in their lists of core values, but many core values are universal: honesty, loyalty, gratitude, generosity, patience and humility. These are the traits that make us good people, people that other people would want to connect with. Connection is the name of the game for us humans! We need to connect with people who are authentic and have core values we respect. That's why we feel bad when we disconnect from people we like. It's a primate thing!

Alan Morinis, in his book *Everyday Holiness*, does a magnificent job on this topic. He brings the study of Mussar to a new century. Rabbi Moshe Chaim Luzzatto wrote a seminal work called *The Path of the Just* in 1740. It contains centuries of lessons to help us live our lives more justly. Morinis explains that although the world has changed a lot through the centuries, the nature of human beings has not changed. We need a guidebook here in the 21st century just as badly as they needed one in the 18th century.

In *Everyday Holiness,* there are eighteen core values—called *middot* in Hebrew—that students work on for one week each in a systematic fashion. When they are done with all eighteen middot, they start over from the beginning. The Institute for Jewish Spirituality suggests reading the chapter on a core value, coming up with a slogan for it, writing it down on a couple of 3x5 cards and placing them where you would see the slogan. The cards will remind you to consider the value on and off during the day.

My slogan for the core value of patience was "Open a space between the match and the fuse." That phrase came directly from Morinis's book and is attributed to Rabbi Perr, who I'm pretty sure was channeling Victor Frankl before him. Frankl said, "Between stimulus and response there is a space. In that space is our power to choose our response. In our response lies our growth and our freedom."

Every night before bed, I tried to journal about the particular core value that showed up during the day. Then I focused on how I handled the situation, hopefully with more balance. Then once a week, I had a phone call with a study partner to discuss how our practices were going. Knowing that I had a dedicated time each week to talk to my study partner made the practice more serious for each of us. We would each speak for five minutes about how, using our slogans and journaling our experiences, we found life during the week. Then we had time to respond to each other and catch up in a broader context about our week. Sharing this way, in such an intimate exchange of hearts and minds, created a very special friendship.

Morinis is actually describing mindfulness when he teaches that you have to know impatience is coming up in your body in order to choose how to react. He teaches exactly what we teach in Mindfulness class—to label the emotion, "Oh, I'm feeling impatient," or "There's impatience." He explains that patience means enduring and tolerating, actually bearing whatever it is, which can bring us a measure of suffering. But that labeling helps to keep a little space open so we can choose a more skillful reaction.

If you are labeling the emotion, you are not fully engulfed by the emotion. Morinis says it beautifully.

> Truth and consciousness are preconditions to exercising free will. Only when the light of awareness is glowing brightly can we see the truth and choose to follow a course that is guided by our values and goals, not our 'animal soul': instincts, emotional reactions, and habits. And the brighter the awareness glows, the more freedom of choice we have. (Everyday Holiness, 60)

Morinis goes on to state that meditation is a technique that can increase the strength of awareness, but it will only be there when you need it if you practice mindful awareness when you don't need it. There's the rub. That's where discipline comes in. I teach my students that this stuff really works, but only if you practice. It is dose dependent. You need to have it so wired in that it is automatic like it is now for me, almost 80 percent of the time.

Equanimity is one of my core values, and patience plays a huge role in maintaining equanimity. My practice of meditation helps me automatically make the crucial pause that is necessary for me to have my prefrontal cortex come on line so I can make a more skillful response.

In the following story, you will see how I flipped into a gentle inquiry on what the heck was going on inside my body. With my Mindful Methods toolbox at the ready, using these techniques helped turn what could have been a nightmare into a peaceful experience, enabling me to stay aligned with my core values.

My family are all animal lovers. We usually have four dogs and three cats running around our house with our kids. A few years ago, we lost our ten-year-old Briard to cancer. It was devastating. My husband thought he was doing me a favor by whisking Shadow away without telling the kids or me and having him put to sleep. I know why he thought that, because years before we had a terrible experience putting our very sick Old English sheepdog to sleep and I had flashbacks for months. I still miss Shadow. Actually, I miss every dog that has ever left us.

About six months ago our bulldog-shihtzu mix, Dusty, needed to be laid to rest. He was seventeen, pretty much deaf and blind, incontinent, and filled with cancer. It wasn't until the cancer diagnosis that anyone in my family would even consider putting the old guy down. My husband was out of town on business when I made the appointment at the animal specialty hospital to euthanize Dusty.

That was the day Dusty could no longer lift his back hips. We were keeping him alive past the point where he could have any joy in his life. My husband called me while I was driving to the animal hospital and asked me to wait for him to get home, so we would be there together, but it was emotional and I was resolved. I had the appointment, so I was going.

In the waiting room, they took Dusty away to put an I.V. in his leg and told me they would get me when he was ready. He would be put in a nice room decorated like a room in a house, not like a room in a hospital. As I sat in the waiting room, I felt like throwing up and passing out. I was actually surprised by my reaction because I was convinced I was ready to do this, and Dusty was more than ready.

What was happening in my body? Closing my eyes I dropped down to envision what was going on inside of me. *That is mindfulness, noticing what is coming up while it is happening.* There was a thick cinder block of vibrating constriction in my trunk, from my chest to my pelvis. I put my hand over my heart and tried Loving Kindness phrases for myself. I still felt the brick but it was a little less solid.

Then I tried a meditation to attempt to soften and soothe the area in my body that had the bad feeling and allowed it to be there, as I had learned to do. Yet I found I couldn't concentrate on all that instruction.

Then I asked myself, "What do you really need to hear right now?"

That did it. That is creating Loving Kindness phrases for the situation at hand. Silently, I told myself I was brave, that I was doing the right thing, and doing it for the right reason, love. Then I told myself it was going to be okay. I assured myself he was a good old guy and now it was time for me to let him go.

A veterinary assistant came to get me from the waiting room and ushered me into a very nice room with a sofa and wood furniture. They brought Dusty, wrapped in a blanket, and laid him down next to me on the couch. He had two little I.V. ports taped onto his left front leg. The doctor explained that the first syringe contained an anesthetic that would make Dusty fall asleep. The second syringe would stop his heart.

The first syringe went in and Dusty started snoring almost immediately. Then the second syringe went in and he went still. Just like that: still.

Looking up at the doctor, I asked, "Oh my God, that's it? Why can't we do that for humans?"

It was so peaceful and so painless. And because I didn't have a vibrating brick in my torso anymore, I could be 100 percent there for Dusty, in the moment, petting him as he passed away.

My compass was pointed due north and I was calm, sad but calm. It felt as though I was right on track with my core values of loving kindness, compassion, truth, responsibility and equanimity.

By creating a slogan for a core value to anchor your awareness during meditation, you give your mind a place to land and focus. It provides you with words that are meaningful for you to repeat and strengthen. If the phrase, or vow if you like to think of it in those terms, reflects your heart's desire, it will have a power all its own.

I love a certain quote about core values, which might be described as the core of one's character. When I was looking it up to read it to my class, I found that it was attributed to Ralph Waldo Emerson, Margaret Thatcher, Gandhi and Lao Tzu. We decided to give the kudos to Lao Tzu because he had come first chronologically! It is as follows:

> "*Watch your thoughts, they become words. Watch your words, they become actions. Watch your actions, they become habit. Watch your habits, they become character. Watch your character, it becomes your destiny.*"

Here is another story illustrating how evaluating core values changed the life of my friend Jill for the better.

JILL

My friend Jill had a high-powered job in banking. She was living the corporate life—long meetings, long workdays, and a big income to seemingly make it all worthwhile. It took a shock to her system for her to realize she was not living in accordance with her core values. Somehow in the climb up the corporate ladder, her values had been lost and her compass was broken. The shock to her system was her diagnosis of breast cancer.

During her leave of absence from work for her surgeries and recovery, she took a long hard look at her life. She meditated daily. She wrote Loving Kindness prayers and recited them every day. She completely cleaned up all her eating habits. She went on a voyage to the center of her being to recalibrate her moral compass.

By the time I attended her party to celebrate her fifth year free of cancer, she was well on her way to her next career. She decided she wanted to help older people transition from independent living to assisted care or nursing care. She had a heart full of compassion for her fellow human beings. She sensed the impermanence of life, everyone living and dying each day. She needed to help relieve the suffering that she could touch in the world. That action element is key. As Alan Morinis explains, "For our response to be truly compassionate, we must not just feel with another person but also try to act on their behalf."

Jill had to go back to school and attend seminars to learn the elder care industry. She knew that helping an older person with that emotional transition involves working with their entire family. She took the tests and received the accreditations that she needed to begin the sales and marketing of her new business. She is phenomenally successful. She puts her heart and soul in her business. Her compass is pointing due north, and she is living the life she wants to live, full of satisfaction that she is creating a difference in the world.

TIFFANY

Sometimes our core values are thrown off by something intangible—not by a job or an event, but by an emotion.

In the case of Tiffany, another student in my class, anger was keeping her out of sync with her core values. She had been holding on to hatred for someone for twenty years. She felt terrible about it because it conflicted with her core values of compassion and loving kindness.

Tiffany had already done a lot of work in personal development. She was part of a large women's group called "The Goddess Group," which holds spirituality weekends once a month. Tiffany had always been able to forgive someone she was angry with by using a gratitude practice to soften her heart. In the case of her hatred of this woman, her gratitude practice—no matter how many times she tried—failed her.

When I mentioned in class that you must get in touch with and slog through the muck of seeing and feeling the pain before you can open to forgiveness, she had an "a-ha" moment. *That is mindfulness—dropping down and experiencing the texture and feeling of the emotion, then going deeper and deeper to get to the bottom of the feeling.*

Often pain is under the anger, and fear is under the pain, and some basic unmet need, like the need to be seen, heard, loved and valued is on the ground floor of your heart. She put her hand on her heart to give herself compassion for having to feel the bad feelings. "The person you are forgiving doesn't need to know what is going on in your head," I reminded her. "For this purpose, you are relieving *yourself* of the toxic emotion of anger. You don't need to engage the other person in the process."

That is my concept of common sense. I know other people might disagree, but it works for me! And it worked fabulously for Tiffany. The next time she was faced with the woman who had been the target of so much of her negative energy all these years, she suddenly felt compassion for her instead of anger. It was as if the weight of the world had been lifted from her shoulders.

After the class was over, she shared with me her gratitude for having been able to relieve herself of that heavy burden. She was crying. She said she felt the heaviness of the weight of anger lifted up and away and replaced with the deep-knowing feeling of compassion that feels like her true home. She never expected to be able to move the needle on her compass with reference to that one issue. And yet, there it was. Her compass pointed due north again, steady as she goes!

MINDFUL METHODS TO CHECK YOUR COMPASS

"Dropping down" to see what's there, not judging it, just noticing with curiosity: this is the heart of what mindfulness practice is all about. It takes practice, but pretty soon after listening to guided mindfulness meditations and practicing the exercises I explain in this book, you will be able to slow down and tune into your body. You will soon, almost instinctively, begin to notice what is happening inside you.

When you feel joy, you will recognize that wonderfully expansive feeling. When you feel anxiety or fear, you might sense a tightness or constriction somewhere in your body. When you feel sorrow, you might notice a feeling of heaviness or fatigue.

Once you notice these feelings, you can work with them. Your goal is not to make the bad feelings go away, but to work with the bad feelings to help yourself feel better. It's my experience that this nuance isn't important in practice. Usually, when I work with the bad feelings to help myself feel better, the bad feelings *do* go away. And that is wonderful! And if they don't go away completely, at least I experience my relationship to the bad feelings differently—as if there's more room to breathe around the bad feelings.

1. **Putting your hand to your heart, so you can tap into the mammalian caregiver response for soothing.** This practice works in so many circumstances that it bears repeating. Evidence shows that putting your hand over your heart, or putting your hand on your body where you feel it, is soothing. It taps into the mammalian caregiver response and releases oxytocin and opiates in your brain to counteract the stress hormone called cortisol, which is

released when you are threatened and are in what's known as the fight/flight/freeze, or fawn (deer-in-the headlights) mode.

This soothing touch calms the mind. In her book *Bouncing Back,* Linda Graham devotes a chapter to the scientific underpinnings of why this soothing touch works. I put my hand on my heart twenty times a day. Whenever I hear a bad story, up goes my hand to my heart! Some of my students found that placing their hands on their bellies or one hand on their cheeks worked better to give them the feeling of love and connection than putting their hands on their hearts. Try all different hand positions and see what works for you. If you are in the workplace, pick a soothing touch that isn't obvious, like holding your arms or holding one hand in the other hand. That way, you can soothe yourself without your coworkers (or boss!) knowing the negative effects they are having on you!

2. **Saying Loving Kindness phrases for yourself.** Remember to say the phrases you've already established as being effective for you. If those phrases don't work, then use the method below.

3. **Asking yourself what you really need to hear right now.** This is a go-to method for me. I like the creativity and personalization it allows me in any given situation. Try making up phrases next time you feel bad and see how it feels.

CHAPTER 7

PRACTICE, PRACTICE, PRACTICE

HAVE I STRESSED enough that you need to practice one of these techniques every day? I mean it, every day. If you skip a day, don't beat yourself up over it. Just pick a one-minute meditation and do it. Everyone can carve out one minute! The guided meditations in the Insight Timer app vary in length from one minute to over thirty minutes. Just pick one, based on the amount of time you have, close your eyes, and follow the voice.

There are hundreds of guided meditations on CD disks and many websites listed in the resource section at the end of this book that provide free, guided meditations to stream or to download. When my mother was ill, I bought her a Sony Walkman CD player and headphones so it would be easy for her to listen to guided meditations without having to deal with too much technology.

At one point, she sent me the following message, "Just finished one hour Jack Kornfield on healing on the CD player you got for me so long ago. Boy am I relaxed!"

I like to do meditations in my car. The seat is just perfect; I can be upright, supported, and comfortable. And I can plug my iPhone into the sound system so the meditation comes through my car radio. If I get to an appointment early, I sit and do a meditation. Easy peasy. Give that active brain of yours a break!

DROP INTO MINDFULNESS THROUGHOUT YOUR DAY

You probably have mindful moments on and off throughout your day. Those count. Pat yourself on the back for those moments. For me, brushing my teeth is a great mindfulness exercise. It's something I do twice every day, and now I consciously brush my teeth mindfully. I close my eyes to limit visual distractions, which makes it easier for me to think only about the feel of the brush on my teeth and gums—the taste of the toothpaste, the sound of the electric brush in my mouth, the feeling of my teeth when I am finished. And I carry the mindfulness through flossing my teeth. So there are three minutes of total, in-the-moment awareness. What a nice break for my brain!

Drinking your morning coffee or tea can be another great mindfulness activity. If you are feeling the warmth of the mug in your hands and smelling the coffee and paying attention to how it tastes when you take your first sip—this is all mindfulness in practice. You might want to drink the entire cup like that, savoring each swallow!

Walking to your car is another time that can be a mindfulness exercise. I'm usually too distracted for this one, but I know it works for other people. Cooking is another opportunity to practice mindfulness. If I remember to pay attention to what I'm doing, I can really get in the groove when I'm stirring a pot or cutting produce. I give my students little, brightly colored dot stickers to place on things in their environments to remind them to pay attention to what they are doing in that moment—and to breathe. I have a little green dot on the dashboard of my car. It's a terrific reminder for me to be right here, right now.

Mindful eating is another helpful meditation. In MBSR, you learn a long exercise on how to mindfully eat a raisin. You look at the raisin, noticing its ridges and color. Then you listen if it makes any noise when you roll it around in your fingers near your ear. Then you finally put it in your mouth and chew it for a while. Then you swallow it. I admit I didn't love the raisin exercise at first; *I mean where had those raisins been? Were those clean raisins?* My son still makes fun of the raisin exercise from the MBSR class that I bought for him when he was in college. (He sent me a video of the California Raisins.) I have to tell you though, I LOVE when I remember to eat mindfully. The food tastes unbelievable. And I find I eat much more slowly. When my friend Monica served the most incredible fresh berries, she agreed when I said, "It's like a crazy party in your mouth."

Because I'm lucky to live in San Diego, I frequently have a walking meditation on the beach. I love to open all my senses to feel the air on my skin, to hear the birds, the surf, and the people, and to see the colors and shapes and sights of the scene. I like to feel my body walking, concentrating on different parts of my feet, legs, and arms, and then switching back to all my senses, taking everything into my awareness. The walking meditation starts by grounding yourself through the soles of your feet.

The soles of the feet exercise is great because it is easy for people to understand and feel. I teach it early on in my class. It's great because you can even do it sitting in a chair. You just need your feet flat on the floor and focus your attention of the soles of your feet. Notice whether your feet are warm or cold, moist or dry, in a sock and shoe or bare. Then you can move your ankles around to shift your weight to the sides and front and back of your feet and notice how your feet feel on the floor. All this foot business keeps your attention on your feet instead of jumping to react to whatever stimulus is presenting itself to your brain at that moment. So to slow things down, and to allow time to have your prefrontal cortex come on line to help you choose a more skillful reaction, you can drop your attention down to your feet.

Another fabulous activity that you probably already do and have never thought of as a mindfulness exercise in daily life is listening to music. If you are really listening and letting it fill you up and move you, you are using music as meditation. And you are rewiring your brain for more happiness. Christopher Germer's *The Mindful Path to Self-Compassion: Freeing Yourself from Destructive Thoughts and Emotions* suggests creating a playlist from songs that evoke feelings of love. He writes, "When we use music to evoke good will toward ourselves, by focusing our attention and allowing loving feelings to arise, it becomes a self-compassion meditation."

He lists twenty-five songs to get your playlist started. His book has been like a bible to me for the years. And the free guided meditation downloads from his website, www.MindfulSelfCompassion.org, got me through many dark days and nights. When I met him at my MSC teacher training, it was as if I already knew him. I said, "Wow, you are the voice I've had in my head for the last four years!"

There are many acronyms to help us to remember to be mindful. MBSR introduced **S.T.O.P.**

- **S=Stop.**
- **T=Take a breath.**
- **O=Observe.**
- **P=Proceed.**

By taking a moment to stop, breathe, and notice whatever is happening, including your own thoughts, emotions and sensations, you can reconnect with your experiences and then proceed with the choice to take a more skillful action.

Tara Brach popularized **R.A.I.N.** as a technique to help deal with emotions, such as like anxiety and stress.

- **R = Recognize when a strong emotion is present.**
- **A= Allow or acknowledge that it is there.**
- **I= Investigate the body, emotions, thoughts.**
- **N= Non-identify with whatever is there. "N" also can mean nourish.**

Non-identify means not running away with the storyline. *Nourish* involves being good to yourself, which may mean placing your hand where you find it the most soothing and telling yourself what you need to hear in that moment. Tara Brach has a terrific website where you can listen to her take you through a R.A.I.N. exercise and have her lead you through many beautiful, guided meditations. I recommend her version of Tonglen; it's gorgeous. www.TaraBrach.com.

Chris Germer created **F.A.C.E**.

- **F=Feel the pain.**
- **A=Accept it.**
- **C=Compassionately respond.**
- **E=Expect skillful action.**

Face your challenges. Feel the pain, don't resist. So many teachers have said, "What we can feel, we can heal. What we resist, persists." Accept that emotion is what is happening with you and label the emotion. Naming the emotion takes the sting away immediately. Compassionately respond to any challenge by giving yourself loving kindness because you know you are suffering. Expect skillful action because you have all the tools when you are mindful and compassionate. You could use any of the skillful actions you have learned reading this book to see whether and how the feeling changes.

PUTTING IT ALL TOGETHER: A FEW RECENT STORIES FROM MY PERSONAL LIFE THAT SHOW HOW THESE TECHNIQUES HELPED TO KEEP ME SANE.

THE BIG STORM

The night of the storm at the Meditation and Science retreat at Spirit Rock, I had the opportunity to pull out my Mindful Methods. I had returned from the store with my provisions, but nothing could prepare me for what happened at four in the morning. A huge bang shocked me awake. My heart jumped out of my chest. Turning on the lamp, I looked around my tiny room, and said out loud, "Okay, you are safe. You are dry. The roof is still above you."

After quickly putting on my robe and slippers, I tiptoed down the hall to the bathroom. No one else appeared to be awake on my floor. When I got back into bed, I tried to calm down and said again out loud, "Okay, you need to calm your system down. You've got cortisol flying around your brain. Your amygdala sent you into fight/flight/freeze and you need to down regulate yourself."

Okey dokey. Now let's see what will work. First, I tried to do a body scan, but my heart was still pounding in my chest. Then, I repeated a few rounds of Loving Kindness phrases. "May I be safe. May I be happy. May I be healthy. May I live with ease."

That was starting to work, to shift what was going on inside my body to a calmer place. Then I wondered whether I could conjure a bra-busting, open-hearted feeling by visualizing sweet memories. Finally, I imagined my babies asleep in their cribs with their little tushies up in the air and their legs tucked under them in child's pose. My chest started warming up.

Then I remembered the home movies we'd watched at Thanksgiving only a few weeks before. My son, Michael, was so adorable. I guess I didn't have the heart to cut his hair so he still had this full head of blond curls. He was toddling all over and had the best little voice and smile. And Danielle held one of her ankles crossed over the other in her high chair like a ballerina.

By now, my chest was radiating love. I started the body scan again and was asleep before I reached my torso!

I learned these techniques without using the acronyms because I do better with the text in paragraph form. But for people who learn well by using acronyms, I think that in the above example, S.T.O.P., R.A.I.N., and F.A.C.E. are interchangeable with each other. I use H.E.A.L. automatically when I experience a good feeling as it trains my brain for more happiness.

MY MOM'S HEART, THEN AND NOW.

In 2003, way before I learned any of what I've written about here, my mom had open-heart surgery. We flew from San Diego to Cleveland so she could see the doctors at the world famous Cleveland Clinic. It's true her case was complicated; she needed a new aortic valve and her heart had thickened Idiopathic Hypertrophic Subaortic Stenosis (IHSS), so it needed to be scooped out a bit. She also had a leaky mitral valve. But she was only seventy years old and she was otherwise healthy, so we hoped for a positive result. What transpired over the subsequent three weeks was a shit show with a capital "S." And I had no tools!

My two sisters, my dad and I sat in the family waiting room the morning of the surgery. After many harrowing, nail-biting hours, they called us and told us the surgery went well and that we should be able to see my mom in the recovery room within the hour. Then she didn't make it into the recovery room. We learned she died on the gurney on the way to the elevator and they raced her back to the OR. While trying to resuscitate her, they accidently blew open the sutures in the big vein in her neck (superior vena cava), where the heart-lung machine had been connected. She bled out and was transfused. There was chaos in the OR, so it's not clear from the charts exactly what happened when, but they cracked her chest open. The surgery earlier in the day had been minimally invasive, but now they opened her like a wardrobe and did some repair work on her mitral valve, the consequences of which plagued her for the rest of her years.

When we finally got to see her in the ICU, she was in a coma. They were unable to control her fluids, so her lungs were wet and her eyes were so full of fluid that her eyelids would not close. My beautiful mom looked like a monster. The surgeon was missing in action for forty-eight hours after that. No, that's not a typo. We didn't hear from him until forty-eight hours after the surgery, so we had no one to explain anything or reassure us. We questioned the resident who had been in the OR at the time of the disaster, and all he could say was they were now worried about her neurological functioning.

I'll never forget that day. My body was in shock; I was shaking and felt like vomiting. Everything inside my body was contracting and constricting. I went outside the front doors of the hospital and called Lowell. I was trying to squeak out words while crying and gasping for breath. I had this tremendous pressure in my head and my throat felt hot and tight. He offered to come to Cleveland, but

I didn't want him to leave our kids. I had no idea how long I would be there or if my mom was going to make it out neurologically normal or even alive. One of her biggest fears was she would get "pump head," which is dementia from being on the heart-lung machine needed during open-heart surgery. Her biggest fears were now a very real possibility.

Lowell had my doctor call the pharmacy at the Cleveland Clinic with a prescription for Xanax for me. That was my *only* tool. My sisters could tell in an instant when I was at my mom's bedside and hadn't taken a Xanax. Even if I was silent, my body betrayed me. They could tell that I was absolutely freaking out inside. So I would go out into the hall, pop a Xanax, wait a while, and come back into the room.

I spent three weeks at the Cleveland Clinic with my parents. My two sisters had to leave after a couple of days. A walkway joined the hotel and the hospital, a sort of a bridge. Every day I would walk like a zombie from *Night of the Living Dead* across that bridge of sighs. I remember being both numb and shaky at the same time. There was no fresh air. I didn't think about walking outside. I didn't think about taking care of myself. Now, with the tools I've learned, I would have known to take a walk in the fresh air. I would have made myself take a bath. I would have kept a list of self-care activities and forced myself to do a couple of good things for myself every day. I teach a unit on empathy fatigue for caregivers in the Mindful

Self-Compassion course, and I certainly would have practiced that material on myself.

Every night, my dad and I would put food in our mouths, chew it up, and swallow it down. I have no idea how either of us ate anything at all. We each drank a scotch or two and fell into some sort of sleep when the time felt right, and the following day, we'd wake up and start over. My mom spent six days in the ICU instead of the one expected day. Just being in the ICU for that long can make people nuts. My mom had one horrible complication after another—everything from respiratory distress, infiltration in both arms (imagine having to put a blood-pressure cuff on your leg because your arms are streaked with red and sore to the touch), and infection in the surgical wound. Once Mom was out of the ICU, a night nurse was stationed in my mom's room. But I slept in her room most nights after she had a bad experience with a male nurse who told her if she didn't stop trying to take her oxygen cannula off her nose, he would tie her hands to the bed. My dad wanted to sleep there, but he had a cold and I didn't want him wearing himself out or inadvertently passing the cold to my mom.

My parents have been married since 1952. It killed me to see my dad suffer when his beloved wife was sick. I have tools now to help me manage that kind of pain. But back then, I had nowhere to put it. I didn't know to automatically flip into a Sending-Receiving or Loving

Kindness meditation like I do today. I didn't know how to ground myself.

After three weeks, my mom was strong enough to get on a plane and go home. She said she had no idea how she was able to do it. I asked a close friend of mine, a doctor, the following hypothetical scenario: If someone throws you off a cliff but then catches you before you splat on the pavement, has that person saved your life? Think about that one for a while! To be clear, it was their mistake that almost killed her, then they saved her life.

We found out about one more souvenir of our time in Cleveland after we got back to San Diego. When the surgeons closed my mom's rib cage, they failed to bend a couple of her chest wires down, so they were poking her in the abdomen from the inside. She had to have surgery to remove them. Really, I wish I was making this up.

When I think back to how disconnected I was from my body during that time, I can't believe it. I had stomach aches, headaches, diarrhea—you name it. I was a colossal mess. I was frustrated and angry at the surgeon and the Cleveland Clinic. I did have a good therapist, but other than that, I didn't know how to heal myself. My future self sure could have helped me!

Now fast-forward twelve years; it's 2015. By then, my mom was suffering from congestive heart failure for five or six years. It was tricky business, but her doctors at Scripps Clinic kept her alive and mostly well for years. During that time, I became a Mindful Self-Compassion teacher and completed dozens of courses in the fields of mindfulness, meditation, compassion and brain science. Not only did I have skills to help myself, I even turned my mom on to a good deal of helpful techniques like meditation and gratitude practice. When she was scared after having a pacemaker installed in her chest, she listened to Jack Kornfield's guided healing meditations on the Walkman and headphones I bought her.

Then in April of 2015, she found out she had colon cancer. Cancer: the one word none of us wants to hear, which unfortunately is all too common in all of our lives. Surgery isn't easy at any age, and at eighty-two with congestive heart failure, Mom's prospects for survival worried us. She survived the surgery. And she survived an infection in the surgical wound and another hospitalization for an infection of unknown origin. Her uncontrollable congestive heart failure almost killed her (through no fault of the hospital). That last hospital stay was horrendous. She wanted to end her life and begged all of us to help her do it. Although she actually looked like she might die, her body was still living. Her systems were still running. She was tired of fighting, but her body was still in the game. *And she recovered! She recovered again!* Six months later, she looked terrific, and she and my dad once again began enjoying a quality of life that to me seemed pretty good for anyone in their eighties.

That time, I survived my mom's recovery by staying on top of my self-care and increasing my meditation time each day. I took baths with bath salts. I called a friend. I grounded myself with the soles of my feet and used the here-and-now stone that I wear on a cord around my neck. I listened to music. I took walks outside. I practiced Sending and Receiving meditation, breathing in suffering and breathing out love and light. I practiced another meditation that breathes in compassion for me and out for others, and I practiced Loving Kindness guided meditations. The Insight Timer App on my iPhone has more than two thousand guided meditations from different teachers in varying lengths and topics, so whenever I became tired of my own voice taking me through meditations, I treated myself to the voices of Tara Brach, Chris Germer, Elisha Goldstein, or one of my other favorite teachers.

And I never once thought about taking Xanax.

MY CHILD'S DRUG ADDICTION, REHAB, AND ROLLERCOASTER TO RECOVERY

This story is so enormous in content and complexity that it's difficult to figure out where to start telling it. Does it start when Danielle is in the womb and I take a drug called terbutaline to prevent her twin sister and her from being born too soon? Or when she starts taking ADHD medication at age nine? Or does it start when she is in high school experimenting with drugs? Any parent who has unfortunately walked in my shoes knows that that a myriad of factors determine why some kids become drug addicts and some kids only experiment with drugs. I actually have a science experiment in my house because my daughters are identical twins—monozygotic, meaning split from one ovum and sharing the same DNA—and though both experimented with drugs, only one became a drug addict.

I have racked my brain to try to make sense of the senseless. I give myself compassion for being human and wanting answers in order to try to understand what the hell happened. And I remind myself that it doesn't matter how this happened; what matters is what happens now and how we learn to support Danielle moving forward. Lowell and I recently accompanied Danielle to an AA meeting in Sausalito, California. Many of you reading this book will be familiar with the basic idea of how these meetings work. But this was our first time seeing a meeting in action. When I heard my beautiful baby say, "Hi, my name is Danielle and I'm an addict," I felt so out of my body.

Everyone responded, "Hi, Danielle. Welcome."

It was like being in a movie and watching the movie at the same time. I felt focused and calm, but underneath the calm I had a sense that my broken heart was leaking. I don't want to seem melodramatic about this heart business, but my heart has been pulverized for the last seven years. I know I have metaphoric patches on my heart from all my good mindfulness meditation and self-compassion practices, and I have new healthy neural pathways made from installing positive mental states and rewiring my brain for more happiness and resilience. But the truth is that sometimes grief leaks out and I would be lying if I denied that it happens.

The Buddha reportedly said we make our own hell by wishing things were different than they are, and I can readily admit that I'm a wishful architect in the underworld. But what parents don't have hopes and dreams for their kids? Those hopes and dreams are expectations. When those expectations are not met, that is when little shacks spring up in my hell. If I'm not mindful, those shacks can turn into houses, buildings, and neighborhoods. And then, when the facts on the ground don't jive with what I expected would happen, that netherworld neighborhood of expectations comes crumbling down.

During Danielle's sixty days in treatment at an addiction facility, we spent four days in a family education and therapy program with ten other families. The experience was sort of like being in a very important and meaningful play, but one that you wouldn't recommend to anyone. During our time in the family program, I learned the addicts carry pain, guilt and shame, among other emotions; and the family members carry pain, anger, sadness, hopelessness, hope, fatigue and more fatigue.

Some of the families had been there before; some of the addicts had relapsed and re-entered treatment many times in their lives. Danielle was the youngest resident in the family program. Because she was only twenty-one, she had fewer years down the rabbit hole of addiction than the other family-program residents. So although her story seemed enormous to me because it's part of *my* life, it paled in comparison to the drama that unfolded during that program each day.

During those four days I used the Sending-Receiving meditation so many times a day, I lost count. I held onto my here-and-now stone to ground myself, and I also found myself needing to ground myself using the soles of my feet. Loving Kindness phrases automatically appeared in my mind. One beautiful woman, an alcoholic, was there because she had relapsed after many years. Two of her young adult sons were there to support her. She shared with the group that her husband had been diagnosed recently with early-onset Alzheimer's disease. Her third son, a binge drinker in and out of rehab and recovery, was not with her. It was so sad. My husband isn't great at remembering people's names, so when we were rehashing things at night, he called her the woman with the red-rimmed eyes. I was breathing in her pain and breathing out love.

Another patient was in rehab because of prescription drug addiction. He seemed to be in his thirties, and his parents were there to support him for the family program. His parents were older, maybe late seventies. It was fascinating to watch the three of them grow closer during the program. Six years ago, his brother committed suicide, and he and his father had never spoken of it until the family program. His parents hadn't known he was a drug addict until he entered treatment. He had tremendous pressure as the surviving son, and he was buckling under the strain.

One resident was there because he was bipolar, and his sex addiction would kick in at a certain time each year. It had happened with such regularity, that he and his doctors had determined it was seasonal. When it happened, he'd behave really horribly and embarrassingly. During the family program, his wife shared that they'd seen the results of his brain scans the night before, showing brain damage in his frontal cortex from a prior accident. She was trying to process the new, shocking information; they were telling her he'd never be able to make decisions on his own for the rest of his life. She was tired. She was weeping. Our group was loving and supportive, so she felt safe and "held" by the group. I used the Sending-Receiving technique like crazy on that story.

One family member was supposedly in attendance to support her mother, but I felt she dominated the group with her own trauma. She told us this was the third time she'd stood by her mom as her mom relapsed and went into treatment. She was with her brother, a nice guy who should have been in treatment himself. The three of them were quite something. She cried a river of tears that week. (Okay, it was only four days, but it seemed like a week—or a month). She shared that her mother had been absent her whole life. Her brother had left the country, so she was "it," the one left holding the bag. She talked about her husband and two young kids. She couldn't speak about her daughter without completely falling apart. Her daughter had been diagnosed with Oppositional Defiant Disorder (ODD) at age four. Her daughter engaged in monstrous acts at school and at home. She said when she looks at her daughter, she sees herself. She told her mom, in front of the group, that she can't be there for her again, that this had to be the last time, and if her mom relapsed again, she wouldn't be there to pick up the pieces.

Then there was our family—Lowell, Cara and me. We were in the family program to support Danielle. Michael couldn't be there because he couldn't miss classes in his first semester of grad school. By the time the family program began, Danielle had been in treatment for forty-five days. After the first seventy-two hours of detox, she received access to her phone every day around four o'clock. That was when the staff returned the residents' electronic devices. And that was around the time Danielle called us every single day. You might think that once your loved one starts treatment, you get a break. I imagined that, because she was safe, sober, and in good hands, I would be able to breathe easier for a while. Boy, was I wrong.

Her mood was highly unstable. The entire time she was in treatment was a wild ride. She had startling insights, like telling me, "I stunted my emotional growth at age fourteen because of my drug use." One day she called and said, "Remember when I used to be a cutter? My drug use is just another form of self-destructive behavior." Another big epiphany took the form of her saying, "I don't like the feeling of being uncomfortable." So now, when that happens and she doesn't have drugs to take the edge off, she needs to learn other ways to self-soothe.

Therapists and educators teach a lot of mindfulness and meditation in rehab, including a specific eight-week course for relapse prevention called Mindfulness Based Relapse Prevention (MBRP) that I really hope Danielle will take some day. Most rehab facilities use the 12-step recovery program from Alcoholics Anonymous because it is seventy-five years old and support groups exist worldwide. Wherever you go, you can find a meeting to attend and a community to support you in your recovery. At its core, the program is based on the concept that addicts need support for the rest of their lives. One prevalent idea about AA is that spirituality is important in the recovery process. The program does talk of God in the 12 steps, and an understanding that in order to heal, you must surrender to a higher power, in whatever form that power is for you.

Personally, I'm uncomfortable with some of the language in the 12-step program. I take things literally when I read, but in attending the meeting, I found the higher power language okay. Really, whatever works for people is what is best. The impression that the community of support was the most important element of the program really came through. AA has many subgroups—a thirty-one flavors if you will. If you want a particular affinity group, you can find it. Other brands of recovery groups also exist, such as the Buddhist recovery group Refuge Recovery and the S.M.A.R.T. program. After twenty years in existence, S.M.A.R.T. recovery is gaining traction among people looking for a secular approach. You will find more types and names of recovery programs listed in the resource section at the back of this book.

As difficult and scary as this was for me, I give Danielle credit for choosing to go to rehab. We didn't need to have an intervention. She knew she needed help, and one night, when my husband opened up to her about his fears, she agreed to go. Once there, she panicked and agreed to stay two days. Then she agreed to thirty days; then to forty-five days; then to sixty days. We were hoping for ninety days, but she just couldn't take the rules and confinement for another month. She was correct that it was her decision, and she had done great work for which we are proud.

She hired a therapist, whom she loves, who has expertise in addiction and recovery. The therapist is helping Danielle build the skills to handle the stress that life dishes out. I'm not kidding myself here. I know there is no way to know how this will turn out. Some people go to rehab and can lead a somewhat or mostly typical life afterward; they can have an occasional drink and not lose control. Other people can be sober for years, have one drink, and fall off the wagon completely, and they will be lucky if they can regain their sobriety.

Some rehab facilities teach patients about something called cross addiction—that using any mind-altering substance can lead an addict back to his or her original addiction. For example, if you were in recovery from an addiction to marijuana, the concept of cross addiction would warn that drinking alcohol may lead you back to using marijuana. That is why recovery programs strongly recommend total abstinence; there is just no way to know which camp you are in until it's too late.

I want to trust that Danielle is in the camp of recovered addicts who can lead a typical life and engage with her peers in moderation. If things go too far again, I want to trust that we will know; either she will tell us or we will notice changes in her behavior. I also trust that she will be able to build a robust life from this day forward. Worrying about what might happen is not healthy or productive for me or for her. When worry comes up in my body, I name it and feel it before dismissing it as not needed. What is happening now is good, and that is something that I can support completely.

That brings me back to the concept of over-parenting and enabling, which surfaced during our time at the family program. I wondered if showing up every week was a form of infantilizing Danielle and crippling her independence? Or was it showing loving support? All three of our kids are unusually connected to Lowell and me. Is this a bad thing?

Danielle had never been away from home before, so when she called saying she missed us and wanted us to come visit, we thought we should be there in person to support her recovery.

Now that she is out of treatment, our intuition is to keep showing up, saying we will support her as long as she is moving her life in a healthy direction. Notice I didn't say the *right* direction! No one gets an owner's manual with the birth of his or her child. We just muddle through it and do the best we can. I thank the Universe that I was introduced to mindfulness through MBSR. And I really have to be grateful that I found it compelling enough to keep studying and learning from dozens of brilliant authors and teachers. I never thought I would thank the Internet, but I must throw it a bone, because some of my coursework has been through online, long-distance learning offerings from the National Institute for the Clinical Application of Behavioral Medicine (NICABM), Sounds True and others.

Because I am able to maintain my equanimity, I am a better parent than I was when the kids were younger. I am less reactive, and because of that, the communication between my children and me is smoother and less charged with emotion, even when issues are in conflict. I can feel compassion for Danielle and for myself as well. And on days when things are bumpy, I can put my arms around myself and say, "Oh, Julie, sweetheart, that was really tough."

I've said it earlier in the book but it bears repeating—naming the emotions as they come up helps provide a little breathing room around them. I highly recommend calling yourself sweetheart or another term of endearment. It cracks me up every time. And cracking up makes me feel better. I recently told a friend that I never imagined needing to use my Mindful Methods ten times a day or more, but that is where I find myself, and the silver lining of this extreme testing is that it works!

MINDFUL METHODS ACTIVITIES FOR STAYING CALM AMID CHAOS

1. **Practice meditating. Download the Insight Timer and pick a meditation to do every day. Pick one that fits into your schedule.**
2. **Ground yourself by using the soles of your feet or your stone.**
3. **Practice mindfulness while brushing your teeth.**
4. **Practice mindful eating.**
5. **Practice mindful walking.**
6. **Practice taking in the good.**
7. **Practice letting music help you be in the moment. Make a playlist of songs that move you.**
8. **Practice the Sending-Receiving meditation.**
9. **Practice calling yourself "sweetheart" or another term of endearment.**

10. **Practice Loving Kindness Meditation for yourself and others.**
11. **Practice mindfulness using one of the acronyms in this chapter until it becomes second nature to drop in and see what is happening in your internal world.**

Unconditional
Jennifer Welwood

Willing to experience aloneness,
I discover connection everywhere;
Turning to face my fear,
I meet the warrior who lives within;
Opening to my loss,
I gain the embrace of the universe;
Surrendering into emptiness,
I find fullness without end.
Each condition I flee from pursues me,
Each condition I welcome transforms me
And becomes itself transformed
Into its radiant jewel-like essence.
I bow to the one who has made it so,
Who has crafted this Master Game.
To play it is purest delight;
To honor its form--true devotion.

EPILOGUE

YOU JUST NEVER know what will happen in life. My husband always says, "Life by its very nature is chaos." I see the truth in that statement. But I feel something different, bigger, and more expansive about the chaos. I see love in the chaos. My slogan, "Life is a wild ride," is the headline of the flyer I use to advertise the course that I teach in La Jolla, California. We can stay on the roller coaster, no matter how crazy the ride. Our attitudes will lead to victory or defeat when things take a dive. If we conduct ourselves with gentleness and compassion, even though we may be taking a dive, we will have a softer landing.

It took a fair amount of chutzpah and courage to write this book. While I was writing, I had several mini-crises of confidence. I wondered, *Will I be criticized or ridiculed by the academic community? Is what I have to share relevant to anyone? Who the hell do I think I am to be putting this out there in the universe?*

When I feel that little kernel of doubt, I think of what Marianne Williamson wrote in *A Return to Love* that basically says go bold or go home!

> Our deepest fear is not that we are inadequate. Our deepest fear is that we are powerful beyond measure. It is our light, not our darkness that most frightens us. We ask ourselves, Who am I to be brilliant, gorgeous, talented, fabulous? Actually, who are you not to be? You are a child of God. Your playing small does not serve the world. There is nothing enlightened about shrinking so that other people won't feel insecure around you. We are all meant to shine, as children do. We were born to make manifest the glory of God that is within us. It's not just in some of us; it's in everyone. And as we let our own light shine, we unconsciously give other people permission to do the same. As we are liberated from our own fear, our presence automatically liberates others.

Ultimately, I decided to go with my intuition and just do it. Thankfully, when anxiety was rising up in my body like a tidal wave, I had the tools to deal with it. I'd often say out loud, "Oh, that's anxiety coming up."

"Oh, that's fear."

"Oh, that's fear of embarrassment, or God forbid, shame."

Then I'd pick a favorite meditation technique and do it. Honestly, I think if you only learn two meditations—the Loving Kindness Meditation and the Sending-Receiving Meditation — those alone can change your life.

The difference between the other authors writing in this field and me is that I am the lay reader, the target audience of this brand of self-help. When I started my journey, I desperately needed to find balance in my life for myself, not for anyone else. I'm not a professor or therapist. I'm just a normal woman who took in what was available, figured it out, and practiced like there was no tomorrow. After a few years of daily practice, the difference in how I view my life is like night and day. And night and day is a good expression because there is so much more light in my life now. Now I teach what I know.

I have a deep wish that you will have at least one take-away from my journey that can assist you on your path to health and happiness. May all beings be safe and free from suffering. May all beings be happy and healthy. May we all live with ease.

RESOURCES

BOOKS AND PUBLICATIONS

THERE IS NO WAY for me to include all the books that inform my journey. I am a woman of the book in the hugest way! So here is just a sample of the books that have impacted me in the last eight years.

Baraz, J. & Alexander, A. (2010). *Awakening Joy: 10 Steps That Will Put You on the Road to Real Happiness.* New York: Bantam Books.

Brach, T. (2003). *Radical Acceptance: Embracing Your life with the Heart of a Buddha.* New York: Bantam Dell.

Brown, B. (2010). *The Gifts of Imperfection: Let Go of Who You Think You're Supposed to be and Embrace Who You Are.* Center City, Minn.: Hazeldon.

Chodron, P. (1997). *When Things Fall Apart: Heart Advice for Difficult Times.* Boston: Shambhala.

Fischer, N. (2012). *Training in Compassion: Zen Teachings on the Practice of Lojong.* Boston: Shambhala.

Germer, C. (2009). *The Mindful Path to Self-Compassion: Freeing Yourself from Destructive Thoughts and Emotions.* New York: Guilford Press.

Gilbert, P. (2010). *The Compassionate Mind: A New Approach to Life's Challenges.* Oakland, CA: New Harbinger.

Graham, L. (2013). *Bouncing Back; Rewiring Your Brain for Maximum Resilience and Well-Being.* Novato, CA, New World Library.

Hanson, R. (2009). *Buddha's Brain: The Practical Neuroscience of Happiness, Love & Wisdom.* Oakland, CA: New Harbinger.

Hanson, R. (2013). *Hardwiring Happiness: The New Brain Science of Contentment, Calm, and Confidence.* New York: Crown Publishing.

Kabat-Zinn, J. (1990) *Full Catastrophe Living: Using the Wisdom of Your Body and Mind to Face Stress, Pain, and Illness.* New York: Dell.

Kabat-Zinn, J. (1994). *Wherever You Go, There You Are: Mindfulness Meditation in Everyday Life.* New York: Hyperion Press.

Morinis, A. (2007). *Everyday Holiness: The Jewish Spiritual Path of Mussar.* Boston: Shambhala.

Neff, K. (2011). *Self-Compassion: The Proven Power of Being Kind to Yourself.* New York: HarperCollins.

Siegel, D. (2011). *Mindsight: The new Science of Personal Transformation.* New York: Bantam Books

Slater, J. (2004) *Mindful Jewish Living: Compassionate Practice.* New York: Aviv Press.

RESEARCH STUDY ON NSSI

Van Vliet, K; Kalnins, C. "A Compassion-Focused Approach to Nonsuicidal Self-Injury *Journal of Mental Health Counseling 33.4 (2011) 295-311.*

WEBSITES

Julie Potiker: www.mindfulmethodsforlife.com

Chris Germer: www.MindfulSelfCompassion.org

Tara Brach: www.tarabrach.com

Jon Kabat-Zinn: www.umassmed.edu/cfm/index.aspx

Paul Gilbert: www.compassionatemind.co.uk

Brene Brown: www.brenebrown.com

Christine Tomasello: www.joyful-coaching.com

Dharmaseed: www.dharmaseed.com

AWESOME SMARTPHONE APPS
When Things Fall Apart – Read by Pema Chodrun.

Be Here Now –Ram Dass. Tons of great articles.

Insight Timer – Guided meditations of varying length from many different teachers. This also offers affinity groups if you would like to connect to other like-minded people.

Omvana– Contains guided meditations and music that you can customize to each track.

E-MAIL NEWSLETTERS AND ONLINE COURSES
If this is the content you read when you scroll through your e-mail inbox every day, you will be positing positive thoughts in your brain.

J.O.T. from Rich Hanson – news@rickhanson.net

Insightful and inspiring, this is my go to newsletter. You will receive information about upcoming seminars and retreats, in addition to learning about his Foundations of Well-Being online course, which is excellent.

Greater Good Science Center – greater@berkely.edu

This organization studies the psychology, sociology, and neuroscience of well-being and provides courses, articles, videos, and other tools for well-being.

Sounds True – soundstrue.com@enews.soundstrue.com
A well- known resource for spiritual wisdom, this site operates a multimedia center, with everything from video, audio, classes, products, and festivals.

National Institute for the Clinical Application of Behavioral Medicine ruthbuczynski@nicabm.com
They run courses for clinicians, but anyone can take them. I've taken many of their courses. If you purchase the course instead of watching it at the time it is streaming live, you can keep it forever in your video library.

Mindvalley Academy – support@mindvalleyacademy. com
The largest publisher of self-help publications, they constantly run free online seminars or webinars.

en*theos – The Optimizer – wisdon@entheos.com
An intentional community of spiritual people and meditators offering programming and e-mail groups.

The Shift Network – Stephen@theshiftnetwork.com
They are all about world peace. They provide incredible video interviews of the peacemakers of our day.

RETREATS
Institute for Jewish Spirituality

They run terrific weekend retreats and also have courses and e-mail teachings.

Spirit Rock Meditation Center
In Woodacre, California, located in Marin County, this is my definition of heaven on earth. I wish I lived up there so I could go there every week for one of their unbelievable classes. I hope to make time to go for a week-long retreat every year for the rest of my life! By the way, it is a sliding scale to make it affordable. (Buddhists do that!)

Tibetan Nyingma Institute
This is in Berkeley, California. It's in a cool house that was formerly a fraternity house. They run all sorts of retreats and classes. I loved it there.

INFORMATION ABOUT ADDICTION RECOVERY:

12 Step and Recovery Groups
Alcoholics Anonymous (AA) (aa.org)
Adult Children of Alcoholics (ACA) (adultchild.org)
Al-Anon.org (al-anon.org) For family members of addicts.
Cocaine Anonymous (CA) (ca.org)
Crystal Meth Anonymous (CMA) (crystalmeth.org)

Dual Recovery Anonymous (UK): A 12-Step Program for those with a dual diagnosis

Food Addicts in Recovery Anonymous (FA) (foodaddicts.org)

Food Compulsions Anonymous (foodcompulsions.wordpress.com)

Gamblers Anonymous (GA) (gamblersanonymous.org)

LifeRing Secular Recovery (lifering.org)

Marijuana Anonymous (marijuana-anonymous.org)

Narcotics Anonymous(NA) (na.org)

Nar-Anon (nar-anon.org) For family members of addicts.

Nicotine Anonymous (nicotine-anonymous.org)

S-Anon (sanon.org)

Sexaholics Anonymous (sa.org)

Sex and Love Addicts Anonymous (SLAA) (slaafws.org)

Smart Recovery (smartrecovery.org)

Women for Sobriety (WFS) (womenforsobriety.org)

XA Speakers (xa-speakers.org) A collection of recordings from speaker meetings, conventions and workshops of 12-step groups.

12 Steps (12step.org) Resources for all 12 step programs. It contains an in-depth discussion and forum on the 12 steps.

12StepTreatmentCenters.com A list of 12 Step treatment centers around the world.

ONLINE SELF-HELP FORUMS

AA Intergroup (aa-intergroup.org)

Addiction Recovery Guide (addictionrecoveryguide.org)

Addiction Survivors (addictionsurvivors.org)

NA Chat (na-chat.com)

Soberistas (soberistas.com)

Support Groups (supportgroups.com) Covering a wide range of issues including: addiction, depression, anxiety and suicide

12 Step Forums (12stepforums.net)

ABOUT THE AUTHOR

JULIE POTIKER RECEIVED a bachelor's degree in general science with a concentration in psychology and theatre from University of Michigan. She then received a juris doctor from George Washington University Law School. She is also of graduate of the Wexner Heritage Foundation Adult Jewish Literacy Program, a two-year intensive course of study for Jewish leaders. She practiced law for a short time in Southfield Michigan before retiring to raise her family. After moving with her husband and young son to San Diego, California, Julie became involved as a leader in many agencies and organizations in San Diego County, New York, and Israel.

Potiker sat on the boards of the La Jolla Playhouse, The Lawrence Family JCC Jacobs Family Campus, Hillel, the Agency for Jewish Education, United Jewish Federation, The National Jewish Book Council and the North American board of the Pardes Institute for Jewish Studies. She was instrumental in creating and building programs and events that continue to this day at Pardes, where she was president of the board, and at the JCC, where she was president of the board and was involved in dozens of programs and initiatives through the years. At every non-profit organization to which Julie gave her time, she was involved in educating the public about the mission of the institution and raising funds.

Julie registered for Mindfulness-Based Stress Reduction at the UCSD Center for Mindfulness, and after eight weeks of training, she knew that a whole new world of education and practice was opening up for her. She began teaching Mindful Self-Compassion (MSC) in San Diego and realized her students deserved all the great teachings from a variety of scholars. Julie began to synthesize her knowledge into her Mindful Methods for Life program, which she now teaches at the Balanced Mind Meditation Center. Potiker and her dad, Paul Jacobowitz, founded the Center at the San Diego Jewish Community Center in 2016, in loving memory of her mom, Ruth Jacobowitz.

Potiker lives in La Jolla, California, with her husband Lowell, son Michael, twin daughters Cara and Danielle, four dogs, and one cat.

Made in the USA
San Bernardino, CA
20 April 2018